AF262711

Tshabangu Sibusiso Malvin

Stars Do Fall in *Love*

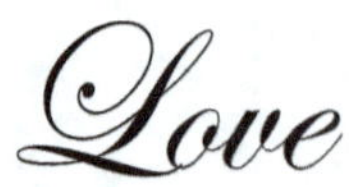

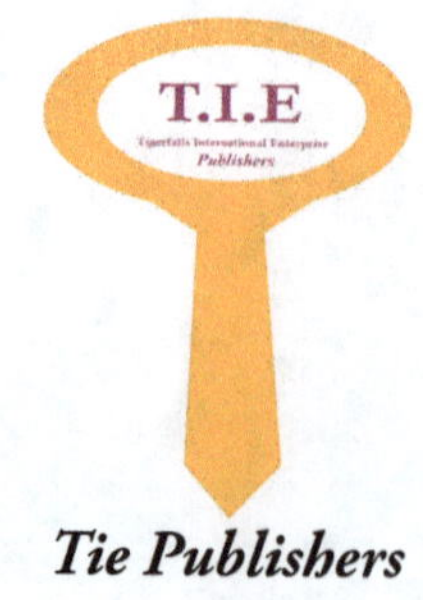

Tie Publishers

The Lady at the Center of my Heart

Dedication

This message is for everyone who desires to make a remarkable impact in their lives. If you've identified a chance to elevate yourself beyond the ordinary and become someone significant, don't allow fear to control you. The stage for expressing your love and showcasing your talents is available to all who muster the bravery to achieve greatness with their unique abilities.

With heartfelt gratitude,

Malvin Sibusiso Tshabangu

Epigraph

In life, after we've achieved all the quests leading us toward greatness, it becomes vital to carefully contemplate and make a profound choice—one that involves committing to a lifelong partnership with the most suitable person. This decision will shape the path you and your chosen partner walk together throughout the entirety of your existence.

With regards,

Malvin Sibusiso Tshabangu

Table of Contents

Foreword

Discovering a groundbreaking idea or invention is no simple task. It's a journey that requires dedication and effort to transform it into a masterpiece. Often, when people stumble upon an innovation, they rush to capitalize on it, whether it's for financial gain or a desire for wealth. However, there's a straightforward approach you can take to reach a point where you can generate the income you need without compromising your vision, idea, or creation.

Imagine you find a way to invent something that the world truly needs in this modern age, but those around you lack enthusiasm or support. Even though the world may clamor to be a part of it, you're the sole champion of your idea, caring deeply about its potential. Most often, these ideas aren't just about serving society or the environment; they begin with your own desires. What do you intend to achieve with your discovery, and what is your primary objective? Is it to excel and leave a positive mark, or is it solely to amass wealth?

The choice is yours, and once you decide how you want to proceed with your concept, invention, or discovery, make it a commitment that you'll stick to unwaveringly. Don't let anyone divert you from your path of creativity. The central theme revolves around nurturing your idea or innovation into a global success, and this entails understanding all the necessary steps.

You'll be astonished by how the world responds to your knowledge if you maintain hope, faith, and a steadfast commitment to building your life around it. Transform your talent into a solid foundation, and don't yield to pressure or challenges. Stay resilient and see your ideas through to fruition. As you do, you'll witness prosperity and profit materializing wherever you go.

In this fast-paced world of the 21st century, we often face numerous challenges that can test our faith and make it hard to stay focused. The global landscape is changing rapidly, with economies evolving daily and situations shifting constantly. Staying resolute amidst these changes can be tough, but if you refuse to be daunted by the circumstances, you can establish a solid presence in today's modern society. Obstacles may arise from various directions, but they too shall pass. By remaining steadfast in your commitment to achieving success, you can weather the storms of life.

Many distractions may come your way, and people may attempt to sway you from your path, but by remaining true to your core values and principles, you can establish yourself as a brand that is difficult to challenge. This process involves building a sustainable and enduring identity that few can rival. To become a leader, you must learn the virtues of patience and unwavering faith. Only then can you reach a level of prosperity where your ideas flourish permanently. Visualize yourself as a successful innovator, nurturing your knowledge and growing a brand or company that is uniquely your own. By dedicating yourself to your ultimate goal, you can achieve remarkable results.

It's crucial to understand that challenges are an inherent part of life's journey, whether you're pursuing a creative path or following a conventional one. These challenges may seem intimidating, causing you to fear that you must sacrifice everything for success, including your well-being. However, you need not fret about being left behind. Sometimes, you may feel like you don't quite fit in or struggle to find someone who aligns perfectly with your understanding. Yet, as you persist, you might discover your ideal partner, someone whose existence is shaped by your wisdom.

Always remember that success encompasses various aspects of life, including love. As you reach new heights, there will be much to celebrate. Ultimately, you will encounter someone who not only acknowledges your achievements but has also strived to attain recognition on the same platform.

Challenges are a part of life, whether it's in your personal life, relationships, or business endeavors. These challenges can arise when your ideas are not yet yielding results and continue until they bear fruit. Dealing with them is key, and accepting that people have their own lives to lead while you pursue your chosen path is important. As you move forward, hold onto your knowledge and aspirations. Stay committed to your goals without wavering. Strive to excel in the field you've chosen to engage in, always looking ahead and focusing on your strengths.

When you take care of something, no matter what it is, it will eventually take care of you in return. This doesn't happen overnight, as it takes time for your endeavors to provide you with the necessities for a fulfilling life. However, once your efforts align with human needs, they can surpass your expectations and break barriers, allowing you to fully grasp your chosen field of expertise.

You should aim to nurture your brand until it reaches a level of understanding about humanity that matches your own. As you do this, you'll gain a deeper understanding of the world around you, and your pursuits will converge. Your brand will become more attuned to people's needs, and you'll become more enlightened about the universe that surrounds us. Continue your journey until you become an expert. Remember, nobody is born with the innate knowledge of how to be the best; you achieve it through innovation.

With the right qualities and determination, you can transcend boundaries and attain unparalleled success. Along the way, you'll encounter various individuals and well-established brands that excel in their respective fields. These reputable entities have reached a level of satisfaction in the eyes of the public, and you can join them. Be patient and wait for the opportune moments when your ideas resonate with others. When you're fully knowledgeable and well-developed, your worth will be evident, and no one can easily buy you out or discourage your level of participation. Wait for the right time when cooperation and mutually beneficial agreements are possible for everyone involved.

We often find ourselves in situations that can be quite intimidating, and dealing with setbacks can sometimes make us feel afraid. It might seem impossible to achieve success when facing challenges on a global scale, and you might even feel threatened by the circumstances of your birth. Your peers may become competitors, presenting physical obstacles that may seem insurmountable. However, these challenges are merely tests of your abilities to become the best version of yourself. To succeed, focus on self-confidence and stay committed to your goals over an extended period.

You may doubt your ability to maintain your motivation and drive as the world questions your every move. You'll undergo transformations, shedding what's unnecessary, and evolving into the person you need to be to attain the life you desire. You'll aim for numerous goals, but in the end, your personal brand's success will be what truly matters. For an extended period, you'll steer your own course toward prosperity, holding the key to your envisioned future. Others may not fully comprehend your journey, as it's your responsibility to bring your goals to fruition. Maintain clarity about your aspirations and make them your utmost priority as you journey toward your desired destination.

This period in your life is unique and will not recur in the same way. It may linger for a while, but it's not permanent, so make the most of it. You must diligently work on your brand until it's fully realized, understanding the critical importance of staying focused on your path to success. Keep your gaze fixed on the ultimate outcomes and place them above all else. Nothing should supersede this pursuit, as the foundation you build now is of utmost significance, and even though it has a finite existence, its impact will endure indefinitely.

Make sure you invest ample time at the very beginning to shape your brand into exactly what it should be. Put your heart and soul into creating a strong foundation that cannot be easily broken. Dive deeper into this journey, allowing your personal ideas to defend themselves against external challenges until they become a formidable entity.

Regardless of the obstacles you encounter, be prepared for the possibility of delays and a long road to achieving your goals. While others may be eager to move ahead in their lives, you might need to stay focused on your own path and self-discovery. This can be painful at times, especially when your chosen path isn't immediately lucrative.

Once you've taken care of all the necessary tasks, you'll find that nothing can hold you back anymore. Your complete focus should be directed inward, as you delve deep into understanding who you are and what you aim to achieve. It won't be easy, but through this process, you'll build a solid brand that transforms into a new way of life. Even the most resistant individuals will eventually grasp the essence of what you stand for.

Preface

As I've journeyed through life, I've come to realize that we often don't adhere to established norms in our pursuit of innovation. This can limit the options available to us when it comes to choosing the best way to create things that impact our world.

A pressing concern is that we should maintain the intended methods of creation, even as our universe evolves seemingly independently of our knowledge, intelligence, and aspirations. This raises questions about the relevance of engaging in innovative projects. Can we confidently assert that we possess knowledge and insights worth sharing with the world, particularly regarding the creation and betterment of human existence?

Today, we ponder whether there remains a place for knowledge, competence, intelligence, and deep understanding. If there is, how long does it take for one's contributions to be acknowledged? While the world advances, those who believe they can contribute to shaping life in a meaningful way may expect recognition for their dedication to humanity. We don't claim to possess exclusive knowledge, but we believe there are ideas yet to be explored and developed for the betterment of our world.

Hence, if you manage to generate such an idea competently, could you be granted a chance to experience a fulfilling existence because of it? At times, as individuals, we can perceive certain unaddressed needs within our surroundings, necessitating the creation of innovations to enhance various aspects of our reality. It's not necessarily groundbreaking or pivotal; what we're attempting to convey is that it could be a concept worth exploring. If it can be realized and given the necessary attention to detail, it has the potential to enhance various facets of our world.

Nevertheless, as a human who has chosen to engage on an intellectual level and make an impact, there may be numerous factors to take into account. Some of these factors may pose challenges and obstruct the path of individuals who have identified an opportunity to globally showcase their talents.

Adapting to the evolving discoveries of the new century can prove challenging. Modernization has become an integral part of the global community, and comprehending the extent of progress can be bewildering. Some situations that initially seemed straightforward may now appear complex. Can you truly decipher the evolving world before you? Life's inclination to make you feel like an outsider, to diminish your sense of significance, becomes apparent in the way the world treats you.

You might start to feel like people are ignoring you, and you could feel overwhelmed by the situations around you to the point where you're not sure what you're doing anymore. The world might try to make you into someone who dislikes others just for being themselves. What I want to explain is that the twentieth century was really tough because it had big goals for discovering new things and there were a lot of conflicts about how to create things. We couldn't do whatever we wanted back then, so you might wonder if you can achieve your dreams even when everything seems to be against you. Can you find a place where you can grow and learn without anyone noticing and trying to stop you from becoming what you want to be?

There are many obstacles that can block your path, and many people who came up with new ideas in this century couldn't handle them. They didn't have the bravery to accept how the world had changed, and they didn't know how to fight against those changes. It was hard to figure out what the world expected from people in this modern age. It often felt like a battle that you wished someone could save you from, but the struggle of creating something new can be really difficult to grasp.

The end result turned out to be really tough with everything happening around us. People's needs have changed a lot, and you might have trouble accepting how much things have evolved, even though some of those changes aren't as bad as you might think. But you might find it hard to cope with the impact these changes could have on your life. It takes patience and faith to break through the barriers of civilization and be creative.

Acknowledgments

I want to express my heartfelt gratitude to everyone who has made it possible for people to read this book. I have always had a strong desire to share this with the world, and I am truly thankful for this wonderful opportunity that has allowed me to finally convey something I've been eagerly wanting to share with the world once more. Thank you once again for granting me this chance to express what has been burning within me for so long.

The Lady at the Center of my Heart

Understanding what to do can provide us with everything we need. But what happens when we can't figure out our goals? What should we do in such a situation, and how can we find a solution? Sometimes, we may struggle to master the tasks life presents us, especially when we're just starting out. At this point, it's essential to pivot and explore new paths, possibly ones that offer similar outcomes to our initial aspirations.

Can the knowledge you possess be as valuable as the experiences life might have offered you when you first began your journey? It often seems straightforward when you've successfully completed your required tasks. On the other hand, is the path you've chosen worth the effort and can it lead you to the financial stability needed for societal acceptance or even the true love you deserve?

Can your own creativity and knowledge sustain you in life, especially when faced with the complexities of the world? Is it possible to thrive independently, without someone guiding you and ensuring your actions align with common sense?

How can you be sure that you're on the right path, and that your choices lead to success in the end? Our own visions, dreams, and goals for the future often complicate matters, but they are also the driving force behind our journey. Being correct in our endeavors is crucial, as it is what is supposed to ensure our success. Straying from the right path can lead to undesired outcomes, attracting misfortune into our lives.

Now that you've taken control of your own chances for success, it might seem a bit challenging to fully grasp everything happening around you. In order to lead a prosperous life, we expect to receive good things on a daily basis. So, whatever we're currently experiencing is the result of everything we've done, including our past failures.

Every time we fail, it has an impact on our lives. Failing at something doesn't usually lead to success in achieving your goals. You might try to explain your current situation, which may not align with what you appreciate about yourself, but it's the outcome of the things you didn't succeed at along the way.

The idea of embarking on the journey towards greatness may be intimidating, but the path to success isn't as difficult as you might think. If you can manage to do things correctly, you could receive something truly amazing in return. Success depends on how you handle failure and learn from it. Consider that throughout your life, you've been determining the outcome of your own life by staying disciplined and focused on your ambitions. It's possible that you've missed out on beautiful opportunities by not realizing this.

The world has a lot to offer when you follow the right path and approach tasks as they're meant to be done. You can achieve remarkable results by mastering the way things should be done. Even if you've stumbled in the past, you're now giving it another try with a better understanding. If you can just concentrate on doing things correctly, you might be amazed by how the universe responds.

You may be doing something you've never tried before, and you may not know the outcome yet. However, if you commit yourself to achieving your goals and focus all your attention on success, you could create a life filled with wonders and become a person filled with love.

It's important to understand that achieving your goals requires complete dedication. Success doesn't come with a set recipe, but if you wholeheartedly embrace opportunities and learn from life's lessons, you can accomplish remarkable things on your chosen path.

You can achieve the results you've been longing for and experience the love you desire. Imagine not settling for something that doesn't align with who you truly are. You might have faced setbacks on your journey, but you can still build the relationships you crave through hard work and understanding. The timing is not crucial; what matters is your determination to become greater and find lasting happiness.

Consider what you're attracting into your life. Are you influencing success or experiencing failure? It all depends on your choices. Sometimes, you may be surprised by difficult situations, but remember, they often start with minor setbacks that snowball into bigger challenges. It's crucial to acknowledge that the outcomes in your life are often the result of choices you've made.

At times, we don't realize that our experiences stem from the doors we've opened. But also, celebrate the parts of your life that bring you joy and acknowledge the areas where you've fallen short. Sometimes, it seems unfair when we see others on a path we didn't choose.

You could have the same chances at a happy life and experience the greatest joys humanity has to offer. The key is to learn from your mistakes and take a new path toward greatness. Recognize where you stumbled, and use it as an opportunity to change your course. Seize your chances for success and accomplish remarkable things, even in areas where you initially struggled.

When you truly pursue success, you won't be stuck forever. Life can present opportunities that lead to your desired destination. It's crucial not to miss out on chances, as time is not always in your favor. Many opportunities lose their value over time. Recognize the importance of seizing good opportunities early on and enjoy your desired path. Youth doesn't last forever. Some mistakes can be corrected, while others cannot be changed. It's disheartening to accept complete failure without a way out of misery.

You can be determined and shape your destiny. You might even become the pioneer of your success, surprising the world. Not all failures mark the end of your journey. If you acknowledge your mistakes and start working hard now, patiently waiting for opportunities and seizing them, you can live your best life. Even when pursuing your chosen ideas, you can exceed expectations.

By dedicating your life to your goals, you can achieve remarkable things and escape the cycle of failure. Accept your current reality of success by excelling in new tasks. Don't deceive yourself by believing in shortcuts; only perfection leads to your dreams coming true.

It's unfortunate that we often lose our way, wishing for better outcomes. When you haven't done what's required, blaming others won't bring happiness. Your happiness lies where you've succeeded, and your suffering originates from your failures. You could have done so much better, and the nature of things can change when you start doing things right, even though it may feel strange at first. You know that you haven't done right.

If you stop blaming people and concentrate on what must be done, you can enjoy the benefits of a good life for the rest of your days. Everything you need is on the path you're on. Don't keep letting yourself down by making excuses, which have no role in recovery. Accepting the truth prepares you for the next challenge, and it goes smoothly when you reach the end of your journey because you'll have more determination.

Pause and ask yourself how many times you've failed and what you've achieved so far. We cling to our successes and try to forget our failures, but that doesn't mean they won't affect us. The world keeps moving in that direction, and it might hold you back for a long time.

What influences love? Could the failures in life have something to do with the lack of tenderness in your heart? You wanted to find greatness in the depths of your heart and be close to someone who completes you. However, when you haven't done well, connecting with such a person might be difficult or even seem impossible. You might feel ashamed to approach such a situation because you can't handle that kind of responsibility right now.

No matter what you've failed to achieve in your journey, it's all part of the plan, and you're not a complete failure. Your past successes will continue to challenge you, but they won't disappear overnight. You'll need to push harder and make things right along the way to reap the rewards.

When something you do becomes a success, that's where you choose to focus your life. Success builds our confidence and points us in the right direction. On the contrary, failure can hinder our journey, making us feel like failures and causing us to lose sight of our ambitions, our desires for love, and our financial goals. Your ability to succeed in what you do determines everything you desire. When your past efforts haven't been successful, it can leave you feeling lost, without a clear path to prosperity.

When you've experienced repeated failures, you begin to understand that not everything goes as planned. But how does this affect us, deep within our souls? It has a profound impact. It can dampen our deepest desires for life, delay us in achieving our goals, and hold us back from finding the love we long for. It becomes a barrier on our journey towards reaching our desired destination.

During your journey, you might stumble upon something that truly resonates with your heart, leading you to realize that this is your genuine purpose in life. However, it's important to acknowledge that pursuing greatness may become more challenging. What you truly deserve and what you are worthy of is closely tied to your accomplishments, and these accomplishments also play a significant role in finding the deep, genuine love you've been yearning for. This kind of love often blossoms as a result of our most significant achievements.

Reflecting on your past, you may notice various missteps that have hindered your progress towards achieving your ambitions. It's essential to understand that nobody is exempt from this universal principle. While we must adapt to our current circumstances, it's also crucial to recognize that there are aspects of ourselves that we cannot change. It's not necessary to be overly harsh on ourselves, as the pressure of accepting our mistakes can be daunting. Remember that much of this stems from what we didn't do well in the past.

However, there's a silver lining. You now have the opportunity to be exceptionally well-prepared and become your own judge when it comes to assessing your progress. Honesty with oneself is key. You can embark on a new journey, one that you initiate for your own benefit, acknowledging that you may not have been precise in every aspect of your previous life. This newfound clarity can pave the way for a fresh start. You can make a decisive turn and commit to overcoming all obstacles in your path, thus bringing your goals within reach.

Perhaps you possess a unique perspective distinct from the views of others. It's possible that you've long been inclined towards embracing a loving approach to life. This prolonged focus might have obscured your awareness of other influential factors in achieving success. Nonetheless, the journey to unlocking our full potential doesn't commence with prioritizing relationships; they should be considered a final step in the path we embark upon. In essence, you shouldn't reward yourself before putting in the necessary work; the true rewards come at the culmination of your efforts.

This journey measures our intrinsic worth by assessing how deserving we are, despite the fact that every individual is inherently deserving of life's abundant offerings. Occasionally, the setbacks we encounter along the way can diminish our self-esteem. However, if you channel your efforts into surpassing the requirements before you, your odds of attaining success can significantly improve.

Drawing from your own unique perspective and comprehension of life, when all else appears to have failed, direct your attention to the ultimate worth you possess. If you hold firm to the belief that your idea is impeccable and you're genuinely dedicated to a noble cause, remarkable achievements become attainable by meticulously attending to every task at hand.

Surprisingly favorable outcomes can materialize from your diligent endeavors, even when circumstances seem far from coherent. This occurs particularly when you've discovered a newfound purpose that encapsulates all your aspirations, culminating in a well-rounded life. When your journey aligns perfectly with your objectives, success becomes an achievable and not overly challenging endeavor.

You might have searched for love in many different directions without finding any. Now, your chances of finding happiness or someone who will give you everything they have in this life might be very slim. All of this could be the result of not making the right choices in the past. However, if you have a clear idea of what truly matters to you and what you want to live for, you can impress the world.

Along the way, you may have lost many things you never thought you'd achieve. There is a place where all our goals are meant to bring us greatness and fulfill our deepest desires. You may have struggled with the tasks we were all given at the beginning, but by focusing your attention on what truly matters now, you can become everything you've ever wanted. You can embrace whatever life has in store for you.

When you strive to succeed and consistently fulfill your responsibilities, you'll be amazed at how the universe operates. Everything you need is already out there, waiting for you. All you have to do is decide to set your goals on achieving whatever the world expects from you. It doesn't matter how you go about it; even with your own objectives, you can achieve remarkable results.

You have the potential to achieve great goals that can bring new purpose to your life. These accomplishments are waiting for you as part of your achievements. The love you've always wanted and that special person who is meant to fill the void in your heart may not have come through other paths that were available to you. However, if you set your mind on this new goal, you may be pleasantly surprised by the rewards it can bring in the future.

Reaching this goal could lead you to the place in life where you want to be, and you might be amazed at how the universe rewards us for our efforts.

We often complain about things going wrong, but sometimes, it's our lack of understanding about our lives that's the issue. Now that you've gained insight into the fact that love, money, and everything you desire are within your reach, don't hold back. Give your all, devote yourself completely.

By giving everything you have, you can make your goals a reality. You may have seen many people left behind because they didn't do things right. It might have surprised you, as you may have believed they deserved the best. However, failure can change our perspective on the world and impact our journey, especially when it comes to achieving our most important goals.

Love can be painful when you're looking for it, and you're not sure where to find someone who cares for you. But don't worry, the universe can guide you if you follow the right path and focus on what it takes to succeed. You could be on your way to living your dreams. You have your own unique journey, and with determination, you can pull yourself out of a tough situation and return to reality using your creativity.

By staying focused on your specific goal, you can achieve great results and live happily ever after through your own efforts. Finding love becomes easier when you've made the right choices. Opportunities are given to us for a reason, and when we let them slip away, we lose something important in our lives, something we may have wanted more than anything else. So, what do you truly desire that you haven't been able to attain? Perhaps you haven't fully committed to it. If you put your heart and soul into it, you can achieve whatever you long for.

Even if success seems far away, you just need to apply the right elements to achieve it. Maybe you're unsure of how to do it, but everything you need is within reach. The key is knowing what you want and how to get there. Be specific about your goals, and achieving your desires depends on your full commitment to them.

The person who holds a special place in your heart is shaped by your accomplishments and the things we have done correctly. However, sometimes we hesitate to take responsibility for our mistakes. We may not want to admit that we can't control everything in our lives. But it's important to recognize that some of our past failures have contributed to where we are now. Knowing this, you have the power to make changes and achieve something truly remarkable based on your newfound understanding.

You can embark on a fresh journey aimed at bringing you positive outcomes, which you are wholeheartedly eager to embrace. You can strive for success in the areas you now comprehend, understanding that our efforts often lead to rewards. To reach your full potential, you must be willing to commit fully and focus on excelling in your chosen pursuits. The life you build will shape your future and define what's remarkable about you, but this can only happen through meaningful achievements.

From the moment we are born, we have goals set before us. If we want to attain what we desire from this beautiful world, we must persevere and conquer each challenge that comes our way. Failing to do so could mean missing out on many opportunities, as we have the potential to make the most of life.

No matter how fortunate you may have been in life, if you repeatedly fail to achieve your goals, circumstances can find a way to confine you to a cycle of change. Something will indicate that you're not taking life seriously, even in matters of love. To fully embrace love and reap its benefits, you may need to prepare yourself. When you seek affection from someone different from your true self, you might inadvertently attract the opposite of what you desire through your hard work. Therefore, it's crucial to ready yourself for this possibility.

In your lifelong quest to find the perfect match that gives purpose to your existence, it's common to attribute setbacks to external factors. We often blame other people's influence on our lives for dragging us down. However, when you've acted appropriately, you should not feel suffocated by anything, especially not love.

While you may hope for a miraculous solution, it's important to realize that achieving your goals depends on your actions. True love, the one that fills your heart completely, demands determination. It materializes when you've given your all to consistently succeed. At the end of your journey, you'll witness your deepest desires turning into reality.

The love deep within your heart, at the core of your being, can be achieved while striving for the best in life. Relationships can falter when you're not in the right place. One crucial aspect that shouldn't be underestimated is the failure to do what's right; it can hinder your progress significantly. Having plans is one thing, but without the means to put them into action, you can't bring them to fruition.

Whatever you aspire to accomplish or desire most cannot come to life without your hard work. Merely desiring something isn't sufficient; you must overcome the challenges that lie along the path to achievement. You must reach the point where all your goals reside, and this requires the ability to manage things effectively. We all possess something within us that can bring our desires to fruition. Failing to attain this understanding can result in a sense of defeat.

Life responds to who we are, and the goals we set only materialize through our interactions with the world we create for ourselves. Succeeding in your responsibilities allows you to navigate situations with ease. Even the love you crave, which defines your ultimate aspirations, can be hindered by your lacking abilities.

Ultimately, we shape our own identity. If you have an unfulfilled need, ask yourself how to reach the place that offers what you desire most. Our life's vision hinges on our ability to achieve our goals. Even the most beautiful dream can remain unfulfilled if you lack dedication and seriousness.

When you truly value creating things and aspire to achieve the best, you must think beyond the ordinary. Nothing happens by chance; we don't rely on luck but on our own abilities. So, it's important to shed the fear that lingers within you as you journey forward, understanding that setting your goals correctly will lead you where you want to be. Even though we may be apprehensive about our own plans, we aim to make the most of the tasks life has assigned us.

However, if you find yourself straying from the path that's available to everyone due to a lack of understanding, what then? Well, you can always start something where you are, defining your own ambitions and pursuing them eagerly. This is an ongoing pursuit of everything you desire in life, and through unwavering determination in your vision, you can attain all your desires. Ultimately, this shows that our goals hold more significance than the obligations life imposes on us through challenges.

By consistently giving your best to overcome the various challenges of life and refusing to be held back by fear or a lack of determination, you can strive to become the best version of yourself. You'll discover that it's never too late to attain your true desires, even though time may seem to slip away, and you may fear wasting your life. The key is to trust yourself and not let the inner beauty within you be stolen away.

Regret won't be part of your journey once you reach your destination; you'll understand how everything falls into place in the end. Even if it feels like you're rushing to get things right, it's far better than never pursuing what you truly love. How can you justify the life you've lived if you know you had so much potential and desired everything the world had to offer? It's challenging to possess knowledge but not have the desire to create; in such a case, you'd avoid living with regrets as you age, watching others live the way you once wanted.

Yet, you can start something and remain determined to achieve your goals, witnessing them gradually take shape. Ultimately, it's the culmination of our goals that defines us, and without reaching our goals, we cannot fulfill our visions. This holds true for everything, even the love you yearn for with all your heart, which can only come to fruition through the same path.

Chapter One

Woman's Rights

Since the dawn of time, life has demanded that women break free from the complexities of the world and creation, entering a realm where they must assert their right to participate. In this domain, they are often relegated to specific roles and rarely offered opportunities to lead endeavors that could profoundly impact human existence or showcase their capacity to contribute based on their understanding.

Could it be that women are naturally equipped to confront any challenge with resilience, readily adapting to life's hardships? On the other hand, being a man may entail grappling with distinct and intricate facets of existence, making it harder to comprehend certain aspects of the world seamlessly. Perhaps this stems from the unique perspective males hold towards the act of creation, potentially influenced by the myriad experiences they undergo throughout their lives.

Life might entail a journey of evolving comprehension for men, with their thoughts sometimes resisting adaptation to the unexpected complexities of the universe. When faced with formidable or seemingly insurmountable challenges, a male often possesses an unwavering determination to effect change. Once a decision is made, they muster every resource and ounce of resolve to reach a resolution, where clarity begins to emerge. This is a trait predominantly associated with masculinity and is less frequently encountered in females – an unyielding belief system that proves resistant to facile modification.

What inspires a person to embark on a unique journey, attempting something that hasn't been accomplished in all of history? What thoughts occupy a person's mind as they strive to uncover something that could potentially revolutionize the world? Could it be that mere existence falls short of fulfilling all their needs and desires? Is there something you yearn for but cannot obtain or figure out how to attain? Do you sense a void within the grand tapestry of existence that begs to be filled? This void not only presents a business opportunity but also bestows the responsibility of bridging the gap within the fabric of creation.

Perhaps it's something profoundly absent from your life that compels you to recognize a pressing need in the world, a need that only you or your solution can address. This recognition, in turn, offers not just a means to resolve your personal challenges but also a way to enlighten countless others about the greater purpose behind the events unfolding in their lives. This newfound awareness opens doors to shaping a future far beyond what was initially envisaged in the current state of existence.

This unexpected turn of events may thrust you into a life you never anticipated, disrupting the clarity you once had about your path and the world before you. Such interruptions could occur due to unforeseen circumstances or influences that shake your perspective, forever altering your course. However, these disruptions, caused by unexpected factors, might well herald the birth of an entirely new universe.

Our world perpetually lacks essential elements crucial to human survival, and a closer examination of people's lives reveals the existence of these unmet needs. Yet, recognizing this gap requires a willingness to make substantial sacrifices, as you delve deeper into this understanding. If you choose to maintain your current state, you acknowledge the risks associated with pursuing a creative path. This path implies that you may endure prolonged periods without vital necessities, underscoring your commitment to serving others.

There are opportunities waiting for someone to discover and explore, offering a chance to make money in life. However, there are certain missing elements in the universe and in human lives, which are not just financial opportunities, but also essential for people to have. It calls for a dedicated individual to work diligently to invent, master, and improve humanity's situation. This effort becomes a way to heal, especially considering the suffering many have endured.

Our understanding of the world can only reach a certain point, but knowledge about the universe can change our perception of everything around us. It introduces a new dimension and a deeper level of comprehension that may inspire us to embrace it, regardless of how challenging life may have been. After engaging with this newfound knowledge, we may refuse to remain stagnant at our previous level of understanding. The pursuit of advancement can sometimes distract us and challenge our beliefs, causing us to seek a better understanding of our purpose.

As individuals, we are part of the world and creation, giving us the power to make positive changes where needed. This is especially important when it improves the current state of affairs that we find unsuitable for everyone. True happiness comes when our vision aligns with our true selves and is also relatable to humanity as a whole. Our vision should resonate with others and reflect our shared human experience.

Often, we find ourselves in a world that we don't fully comprehend, and we create our own understanding to navigate it. However, we continually face challenges that seem to obstruct our path, as if they will always stand in our way. It's important to reflect on these challenges and recognize what we cannot tolerate on a daily basis.

Sometimes, you might find yourself trapped in your own thoughts and creations, pouring all your energy into making them come to life. As you watch your world slowly fade away, it's not that your efforts are a failure, but rather that escaping from your own thoughts can be challenging. Whatever you try to avoid on one side of life tends to resurface on the other, leaving you feeling stuck in one place. Time keeps moving, and your success depends on your ability to grasp the fundamentals of being a regular person. This can make it difficult to navigate daily life, and you might become frustrated with your existence.

To break free from this ordinary world and explore uncharted territories, it's a journey reserved for individuals and their life's purpose. We must acknowledge that as you delve deeper into understanding, much is taken from you, and you're set on a unique path. Even if you once enjoyed what you were doing, the pursuit of purpose can steal that joy, leaving you with questions meant solely for your chosen path.

When you engage in creative work, you must accept that you're largely on your own. Others, particularly women, may not grasp the significance of your endeavors, as their focus is on the flow of life, moving with the world's current.

Hence, every quest for understanding demands sacrifices, often involving your own happiness and love. Even geniuses can grow weary and realize the importance of preserving their inner essence. Regardless of your stage in life, relationships can challenge everyone, and it's important to allow people to share their true selves, no matter their quest for understanding.

Love is something we all need, even when life takes us down different paths. Sometimes, we all crave a little care and time with someone special. But if you stray from your true self into a challenging journey, it's like losing your only route to happiness.

Sometimes, we're meant to walk a solitary path towards our destiny, where the universe molds us and tests our character. If you truly believe in your mission or have found a unique purpose, you must stay ready for whatever challenges may arise. Keep your intentions clear and remain dedicated to the well-being of all humanity.

It can be quite challenging to be a person who has discovered a unique and special purpose in life. The journey to bring this purpose to fruition often demands a great deal of dedication and endurance. One must invest a significant amount of time and effort into making their dreams a reality, and sadly, love may sometimes have to take a backseat. This doesn't mean that relationships are unimportant; they certainly are. However, if a relationship lacks genuineness, it may not withstand the trials that come with pursuing one's creative calling.

Feeling the pain of transforming intangible ideas into tangible reality can be overwhelming. The process requires unwavering faith and patience as one's understanding takes shape. Giving life to a concept, especially in a world where people are focused on their individual objectives, can be a formidable task. You cannot blame someone, especially a woman, for not always being ready for love in such circumstances. They deserve happiness and beauty without the complications of the universe. Their responsibilities often revolve around the creative process, which doesn't demand as much from them. This doesn't mean that relationships are impossible; they can happen. It just means that finding someone who aligns with your specific purpose becomes essential. There is always a person meant to join you on your journey, someone who shares your perspective and appreciates your efforts.

Navigating this situation involves understanding that engaging in a creative endeavor may come with unforeseen challenges and sacrifices. As you progress, you might witness your life becoming deeply intertwined with the creative process, and at times, it can feel like you're losing a part of yourself to it. When you've given your all and your success hinges on this endeavor, you become fully committed. It becomes your sole focus, the only thing you know. Then, as you emerge from this immersive experience to witness your creation come to life, you realize that you've been completely absorbed by it.

You may find it hard to believe that things might not be as tough as you first thought when you begin a journey. However, once you've committed to it and can't turn back, you start to realize all the challenges that lie ahead. When you dive headfirst into a long-term project, you must be prepared to face every obstacle that comes your way.

We often question why we embark on projects that don't bring us happiness. What are our goals when we knowingly engage in something that doesn't improve our well-being? How long does it take to realize that you're not winning, yet you persist in believing in your initial idea and ultimate goal? Even if given a second chance to lead a different life, would you still refuse to give up?

Perhaps you're driven by a need to prove something to yourself, and achieving your desired outcome means everything. Even if it requires sacrificing a part of your identity, you know that going back is not a sensible option. Progress is the only path to happiness. So, for the rest of your life, you'll follow that chosen path, even though you could have chosen a more conventional way of living, which is typical for humans. You'll forever regret the person you could have become through other survival strategies, but the version of you now is the best possible one.

To fully commit to a certain path, you must proceed without wondering what could have been. You'll never know, no matter how tough life gets along your chosen route. You may wish to turn back time, but that's impossible, or pretend you have no knowledge of the seed that was planted in you. Whatever has planted that seed will continue to nourish it until it grows deeper and stronger.

Many times, we encounter situations where we struggle to comprehend why things have become so challenging, and most importantly, how these challenges impact our overall perspective on life. These circumstances can shape our character, and often, we believe ourselves to be capable of handling whatever the world expects from us. Along this journey, we may even question whether we were destined for a particular path or if we are fulfilling our self-imposed responsibilities. If we believe we've been called to a certain purpose, there may be moments when we wish we could have declined, yet we didn't; we accepted the role of being a solution in the grand scheme of creation, and our path will unfold from there.

In life, individuals, regardless of gender, bear the responsibility of making a positive impact on the world, no matter how seemingly insignificant. Men are subjected to the process of evolution, often rooted in one place for extended periods, striving to influence the universe. In contrast, women are bound by the passage of time, consistently adapting to ensure the planet's well-being. Each person serves a unique purpose; men aspire to correct and gain recognition, while women are driven to flow with the rhythms of life.

The complexity of life can be challenging to grasp, yet this is how the world operates. One can choose the easier path and settle for what's readily available. Everyone desires to accomplish something remarkable and be genuinely appreciated for their contributions. We yearn to alter the course of the universe, break down barriers, set records, or become an integral part of history. Accepting this as our newfound reality requires us to extend our horizons, surpass our limits, and strive for new frontiers; otherwise, we'll remain stagnant.

If we don't pursue these goals, satisfying our curiosity and reaching higher levels of understanding, we'll forever remain ordinary. When we encounter setbacks, the lessons of life can become muted. Failing at something may lead to ongoing difficulties in navigating life's challenges. The moment we lose hope in a particular idea, we risk giving up on everything we strive for along the way.

When you finally fully grasp a world you know so well, it isn't an easy journey for anyone to undertake. But take pride in your newfound understanding. Sometimes, we must ponder whether we appreciate today's state of affairs, influenced by our strong desire to attain our deepest aspirations. Our actions do ripple through society, after all. So, regardless of the universe's evolution, what motivates a person to persist — is it wealth, affection, or the anticipation of witnessing the fruits of their labor?

Life can take unpredictable turns when you've set your sights on a particular goal. Along the way, you may realize you're on a solitary path. Not everyone will be invested in your pursuits; people are busy with their own lives, and this is what defines an individual's purpose. At the outset, it may seem like the whole world understands and supports you, perhaps even cherishes your endeavors. Amidst it all, you're united by a shared objective.

What do you think is the most preferable course? Living life while comprehending your actions or discovering early on what you truly love? Without delving into the complexities of this world, allow the realms of creation and knowledge to be explored by those who seek them, while you find a relationship that aligns with your worth. With the intention you hold now, true love may bloom in the future, with someone who is heading in the same direction as you.

It can be challenging to find a partner who shares your chosen path, particularly when you haven't reached your destination. But as you succeed, a world shaped by both men and women unfolds. Often, we traverse separate routes, and along the way, it may be difficult to spot someone who shares your vision. Such love tends to blossom only through achievement.

Your choices largely reflect your character, as you may be the only one completely certain of your actions and their impact on your well-being. Recognize that much will change over time, contributing to the person you become. Many of your decisions will need to be prudent due to the gravity of your chosen path, rendering the various distractions along the way inconsequential.

You should search deep within yourself to discover your most important qualities and prioritize them. The world has evolved into a more complex place than it once was. Keep in mind that many things will come and go, and they may not be relevant to your life's purpose.

As a man, you may find yourself navigating a universe that demands you to define what you are living for. On the other hand, the experience for women has been different. If you are a woman, you are free to utilize the resources available to you. Your potential knows no bounds as far as the world allows, and you may gain recognition by aligning with predefined goals. However, if you can set aside distractions and concentrate on your predetermined path, you will expand your understanding, which should be sufficient for women.

Men are not isolated islands; they also need love and companionship. Thus, women have the right to benefit from the achievements of men. At the end of the day, no one can live in isolation. It is expected of you as a woman to fit in and make an impression, demonstrating your capabilities, even if you come from a simpler world. For those men who have chosen to lead, the path may have been challenging, but they must not discriminate against those who follow them or complain about their role in people's lives, particularly women.

It is possible that, in the end, you will need to find meaning in the path you have chosen in life. However, if your desire for greatness obstructs your way, it may take a long time to discover true love in your chosen purpose. The more ambitious your goal, the farther you may be from finding someone who will bring meaning to your efforts.

Considering the challenges awaiting humanity, it is essential for women not to be burdened with such tasks. Why? In light of the harsh realities, women should have the freedom to live their lives without undue obligations. Pursuing a goal to its completion is one of the most demanding tasks imaginable, and doing it right matters more than anything else.

As a man, you may find yourself pondering the meaning of life within your own being. The world often questions your authenticity and values. Have you discovered your true self, the one uniquely crafted for a special purpose? Women, on the other hand, seem to possess a remarkable ability to embrace reality, allowing everything to find a place in their hearts and sow seeds of understanding in the present. They are intertwined with the future, and it's a unique experience to recognize the opportunities the universe has presented for personal growth.

Believing in the uncharted, being the trailblazer, or striving to achieve remarkable feats defines one's identity. Women may not always grasp the abstract, yet they hold the key and crown to the current moment, prioritizing happiness as they navigate existence.

We all bear the responsibility of living up to our fullest potential, understanding our actions and their consequences, which truly distinguishes one person from another. It can be even more challenging when you yearn to share your personal journey of self-discovery, realizing that having a clear purpose simplifies life's complexities for all to comprehend.

Life's peculiar design, which places love predominantly within women, raises questions about its tranquil nature compared to the tumultuous paths often pursued in the quest for greatness. These pursuits can lead to chaos and destruction, qualities you might find challenging to accept in others. Instead, you seek companionship with individuals who prioritize caring for others and nurturing true love.

Where can we discover love, that wonderful feeling that's simple, strong, filled with joy, and so inviting? Could it be that everything that makes us who we are resides within us, and some of it requires nurturing? Is it possible that venturing into unfamiliar territory might cause us to lose our sense of self? It might seem challenging to believe that the journey to greater self-awareness and self-discovery is mostly entrusted to humanity, and there's no way to avoid it. If you are destined to explore life more deeply, then you must forge your own path. Could it be that we have reached a point in our lives where we fear solitude and struggle to find new ways to connect in this modern society?

Have we found it essential to take our relationships seriously, devoting our entire selves to them, unwilling to let anything come between us and love? If true love has always been vital and something we should have considered from the start, rather than something we learned to cherish out of necessity, then perhaps people are afraid of a life without it, as this world becomes unbearable without love. Imagine not wanting to be late in discovering someone who truly loves you, as a worthy partner may have been on their own journey, and we cannot deny others the chance to experience love in their lives.

You also need to be punctual; you can't spend your entire life assuming that a worthwhile relationship will wait for you. Love doesn't wait for anyone. You must be timely; you cannot be late. True love, when it's genuine, requires early dedication.

Where does it all originate? Perhaps it's rooted in the human mind, in our confidence in what we do, giving us the strength to handle life's challenges. Balancing long-term goals with the pursuit of love, which holds more significance? Striving to maintain both aspects while achieving the best in everything life offers. As time passes, the big projects that once seemed crucial may fade away, but ensuring that we don't hinder others from finding true love becomes increasingly important. You'll want to know that you've made the enduring choice of marrying the right person.

While your past may shape you, it doesn't solely define you. Your future identity can be something entirely new and greater, determining who you'll become tomorrow. This is the most thrilling aspect of life and love. You can emerge from situations that no one could have foreseen, and that newfound knowledge can be your greatest treasure, propelling you to new heights through pure and profound understanding.

With this kind of intelligence, you can achieve a life that's nearly perfect.

You can have high-quality relationships with someone who truly deserves your efforts. People should always strive to do their best to get to where they are. That's what love is ultimately about – loving everything about each other.

Even though understanding each other might feel like a small community, there are moments in life when you can truly feel like you belong. Along the way, you'll encounter challenges, and you can't simply be vulnerable to everything that comes your way. You need to protect yourself from all the external influences. You can't be subjected to every situation.

This raises a question: does it mean your partner doesn't care about you if they weren't there from the start of your life journey? Does it imply that you can't truly love someone with your whole heart if there was no one to guide you toward greater understanding? Are there situations that you must face alone, and does this undermine the need to love each other, considering we can't solve all of life's problems together?

Perhaps, for men, it also means something significant. You may find it challenging to devote yourself completely to a woman who didn't play a role in shaping the person you've become or offer support. Only if she has supported you in every aspect of your life can you dedicate yourself to such a loving and kind-hearted person. Maybe you deserve better, and if you failed to be with someone worthy, someone else might offer pure and innocent love. If you don't look back, you might discover the value in everything you've been through.

Is it that love deserves more? Do women have the right to distance themselves from you when you're struggling to become the person you want to be? Love should always remain free within our lives. At one point, you might have hoped that someone would love you beyond what's expected, considering your ideas and vision. However, it often becomes a source of confusion for both parties. People want to fall for someone with a clear path, someone who makes sense when you need the right person.

Love becomes real through the ideas we hold. As you gain a deeper understanding of yourself, your value in life increases, and you cherish every aspect of who you are. Think back to the beginning when you weren't fully aware of your actions and may have been your own worst enemy. You weren't battling the world; you were fighting against yourself. As you gain clarity, everything falls into place, and life starts to make sense based on your purpose. With this clear perspective, you can move forward in life without sabotaging your chances of happiness and true love.

Chapter Two

Beckon

Knowledge beckons from afar, appearing deceptively simple, yet gradually, we find ourselves grappling with the complexities of love and its challenges over time. Now, as we embark on this realm of knowledge and creativity, we encounter numerous perplexing and essential concepts that, if left misunderstood, can lead to a life of deprivation and solitude. You see, there persists an ongoing quest to address the world's persistent issues, and a continual hunger for fresh perspectives and intellectual contributions to enhance the human condition.

We have never encountered the ideal scenario where the world resembles a path of creation that not only reshapes your thoughts but transforms your entire understanding into something entirely new. Such a transformation may prove daunting to adapt to, once you've embraced this current way of life.

Often, we venture forth without realizing that the world may have overlooked critical aspects of life, leaving them unresolved. Nevertheless, for those willing to explore this universe of knowledge, the opportunity to unravel the mysteries of existence lies ahead. This journey is a choice, and no one should be held responsible for the challenges one may face along the way. It's possible that the world failed to address this crucial aspect of humanity.

Approach this journey prepared for anything, and once fully committed, when there's no turning back, you'll navigate the path of creation. It's our thirst for knowledge and life that binds us to this transformation, necessitating that we tread this path. What the world doesn't comprehend will require us to make sacrifices to continue our lives as we know them, for failure to do so could close the way for all. As human beings, we must traverse a narrow passage filled with life's greatest sacrifices, which you can circumvent if you find your unique path to understanding.

As individuals, we are not denied the opportunity to live and love, but it's essential to recognize that a repetitive routine isn't the only way to experience life. We don't have to follow the same path to success; while we may study similar subjects, we are not bound to pursue a single field for our livelihood. Some aspects of our lives, like relationships, the need for love, basic human needs, and comfortable housing, are common desires shared by most of us. However, what truly distinguishes us is our unique passion for creation.

Indeed, as individuals, there are certain similarities in our lives, such as our choice of careers as a means of survival. Yet, deep within, there exists a profound difference in how we embrace life, and this distinction arises from our individual participation in the world, which shapes our unique understanding.

Could it be that relationships would pose fewer challenges if we didn't enter this world of creativity? What transforms our responsibilities towards caring for one another into a drive for understanding and prosperity, sometimes leaving love behind? Humans are inherently inclined to connect with one another, and this inclination remains unless profoundly disrupted by an overwhelming force that diverts our focus solely towards survival.

It appears that, over time, creative knowledge is the force that has the most significant impact on human behavior and our interactions with one another. What resides within this realm of creativity and understanding that alters a person so profoundly that they become impervious to external influences, especially in matters of love, isolation, and their outlook on life?

It's as if the universe continually delves deeper into the realm of creativity, inviting us to question life and love in a world where understanding transforms us into entirely new beings. This transformation, fueled by intelligence, is an inner process that brings contentment through silent contemplation. Could it be that our beliefs and knowledge, acquired from books and other sources, shape us into the beings we become, giving birth to our transformed selves?

A new creation, born from knowledge rather than love, might have disrupted or even extinguished the person you once were. You were initially molded by a world filled with affection, arising from the deep bonds between people who cherished and cared for one another. Are you still carrying the legacy of that human devotion within you?

What transpires when a fresh human entity emerges within us, brimming with profound wisdom, ready to surpass conventional expectations, and yearning to uncover new layers of existence, all while striving to leave a lasting impact on the world? Nevertheless, you may find yourself overly committed to your unique cause, the path you've chosen as your form of engagement. On occasion, it will not be an easy journey; you must transcend further and assume a distinct persona that truly distinguishes you.

Despite our relentless pursuit of knowledge, there exist individuals who are designated as the guardians of the universe. They possess comprehensive knowledge and bear the responsibility of safeguarding life itself. Our existence relies on them, and they are entrusted with the duty of ensuring that we remain shielded from all threats in our current reality.

It's a coalition of individuals leading the universe toward a new trajectory, venturing ahead of their time. Yet, once in a lifetime, you might find yourself vanquished by a formidable challenge that leaves you disheartened, with only one person standing firm to prevent the world from losing its way as an integral part of creation. It becomes a man's duty to ensure that he fulfills his obligations and refrains from sacrificing any part of his life in pursuit of normalcy. There will come a time when you must sacrifice as part of the commitment you've made to effecting positive change.

In the grand scheme of creation, there are moments when progress seems impossible for humanity. It is then that someone must step forward to unlock the path, allowing the world to resume its journey toward well-being. At such times, you may ask yourself what obstructs the path to a fulfilling life and why such a route to greatness is barricaded. How does one devise a strategy when the road is impassable for everyone?

The solution requires someone to transcend their usual duties, crafting an idea that precisely outlines the necessary goals or providing a much-needed remedy to heal the world and propel it toward the future. These are the circumstances in which you risk losing sight of your true self, pondering what diminishes the tenderness of life and love in the face of such challenges. What has the power to touch us in our most vulnerable moments?

It might be that the solution requires someone to pass through a challenging journey, and those who successfully navigate that narrow path become part of a newly created world. This individual not only provides strength to you but also becomes a fundamental source of strength for the entire universe, adding meaning to their own life in the process.

A star is born within this person as you gain a deep understanding of the profound connection formed through your tender union of hearts. While every purpose may have its unique demands, some objectives remain undefined while others are clearly delineated. Achieving success often demands a person to sacrifice their identity and the comfort of their daily life. However, love and life are not lost in this journey; they await you at the end.

When relationships become the sacrifice, what matters more than that? When your objective becomes your top priority, what did you give up with love, and what endures? Can you rediscover happiness along the way, or will the joy you seek only materialize when you reach your destination?

Some paths are pursued by few, leading to objectives that set you apart from the rest, often emerging when no clear path seems evident. As the world appeared to falter, seeking salvation from those who believe in an ideal universe or a life path became crucial. This pursuit can earn you significant recognition and define the purpose you represent. It's possible that humanity needed to progress further or address the consequences of its limited understanding, creating a reality we cannot accept.

Often, we find ourselves correcting mistakes resulting from others' lack of comprehension. Despite what may have been lacking or problematic, it wasn't enough to halt the world's progression. Creation continued elsewhere, allowing most people to carry on with their daily routines. Discrepancies in our lives can disrupt the harmony of our reality, altering our perception of what truly matters. What we once considered right in our daily lives may need adjustment to prevent humanity from being misled.

Many may remain stuck, believing that their current situation is the only reality, oblivious to the potential for greatness and progress. Something has unsettled them, and it requires correction. They are so bewildered that they struggle to return to reality, holding onto the belief that the world isn't what they once perceived.

However, if you are out there, living with truth, belief, and faith in a perfect universe, you can be the solution to everything that deviates from what must be.

You must allow the purpose of your life, the one you believe is important for humanity, to come into the world, no matter how challenging it may seem. Do not let anything hinder you from fulfilling your destiny and making things happen. It holds great significance, even if the sacrifices required are greater than what you can endure. Remember, you are not meant to give up; you are here to offer hope. Therefore, you must make it a reality and harness the goodness within you. If your current circumstances align with your aspirations, nurture them. Although it may feel like a formidable battle, strive to bring your dreams to life.

Balancing your love for someone special with your future goals, projects, and responsibilities has always been a tough task. There's no pause button to create a meaningful life that encompasses all that you are. When challenges become overwhelming, you might question the meaning of it all. You are driven by a purpose, even if it seems elusive at times, and you must sustain it with unwavering faith. The people you hope will appreciate your efforts may not currently be pleased with your choices. Consequently, you may find yourself tirelessly explaining your actions to the world, even when it's unnecessary.

You pour everything you are and even what you lack into your endeavors, even when it feels incredibly demanding. You push yourself to the limit, until finding any luck in life becomes seemingly impossible. Despite becoming a force to be reckoned with, you continue to strive, recognizing that there's no turning back. It's your only path to remaining human. You know yourself better than anyone else, and you deserve to invest in yourself more than you've ever done before, as the rewards are immense.

When you commit to a particular ideal project, your life can become compromised. In the midst of it all, you may have felt less significant, as if you've taken a hundred steps backward in order to embrace a new way of doing things. You no longer feel like your natural self, and the personal growth you've achieved may seem meaningless. Yet, there's a part of you, a childlike spark, that yearns to thrive and be nurtured.

In order to make your idea a reality, you must prioritize it above all else, and one of the most important aspects of this is love. You've come to realize that love is a significant part of human nature, and it requires commitment. You can't just enter and exit it casually; it demands your focus and dedication to please each other. However, circumstances have weakened your commitment to love, even though it's not your intention to avoid it.

Something else has taken precedence in your life due to the situation you're in, and the only solution is to continue moving forward. You can't turn back now, and the success of your project becomes the ultimate benchmark. You've let many things pass because you hold a lot of goodness in your heart, and time has become a precious and critical resource that you don't want to waste.

When time is of the essence, how do you effectively manage your responsibilities? You must persevere in the journey of life with determination, always striving to see your purpose fulfilled. You reflect on how much of yourself you've already given to this cherished goal. You've poured your heart and soul into it, even when it got tough. There's no turning back; challenges only motivate you to keep moving forward.

You have two choices: surrender to failure or strive for greatness. Everyone desires understanding, but true recognition, the kind that gives your life meaning, is elusive. The only path forward is one guided by understanding. When you understand what you're doing, you become better at it, knowing how to make the right choices. Discipline becomes crucial because you must complete what you've started in order to reach the other side. Despite the looming threat of time running out, you don't quit until you've seen through all your endeavors, driven by the unknown rewards that await.

Life requires understanding, and it's better when you start well. Sometimes, you break through a certain subject, and that's the most important thing. Your job then is to study more about what you've discovered. That becomes your ultimate goal. However, if you focus too much on one part of your project, you might struggle with other aspects of your journey.

Missing out on love can be very sad. You wish for care and a chance to experience it, but it never comes your way. The joy that others have in their youth passes you by, and you realize you haven't had many opportunities to enjoy life. Your daily well-being is guided by a path that few can truly comprehend.

One of the biggest disappointments is giving up on a project before reaching the end. You quit, and the wonder of what could have been haunts you. On the flip side, quitting can also bring some relief, as you no longer carry the burden. Sometimes, you succeed even if you don't reach the end because you've gained valuable knowledge.

The world can be tough, and finding a place to rest is challenging. Along the way, you encounter things that hardly resemble a fulfilling life, making you question who you're trying to please. Is it about you, or is it about uncovering the truth about our reality? Sometimes, you might not feel like continuing, but then you wonder, who does it matter to? What purpose do you serve? You serve the truth and the world of honesty that defines you. You've reached a point where you've accepted everything you've become. It's not always about us; sometimes, we work for a greater purpose that requires determination to achieve.

Being stuck in between times, with no clear meaning to anything or anyone, can be disheartening. You watch the world move forward while you stay still. However, your journey is fueled by courage and motivation. What gives you the strength to navigate through life? What boosts your self-esteem, enabling you to keep working even when you don't see immediate results but believe in your ideas? What spreads the message of hope, encouraging you to venture further than any human has gone before?

We often find ourselves grappling with an ongoing struggle, uncertain of the ultimate outcome. Nevertheless, we carry a steadfast confidence that transcends mere human patience. What do the outside world, our loved ones, and close friends think of us? When we gaze upon them, how do we perceive ourselves? Or do we simply contemplate all our actions? This is a common aspect of our human nature – the desire to be recognized for something truly remarkable. However, when we immerse ourselves in the pursuit of love, reality can turn unbearably cold and perplexing. It dawns upon us that we tread this creative journey alone.

As we venture into the realm of knowledge and understanding, we often encounter deviations from our envisioned path. We pause and ponder, 'How did I become entangled in this life?' There will be circumstances attempting to drag us down, and people seeking to mimic our identity, all in an effort to hinder the realization of our vision and conceived ideas.

Everyone seems to capitalize on our endeavors, striving to prevent us from reaping the rewards of our wisdom, as if we lack intelligence. By choosing our own unique path, we may temporarily appear unimportant or unintelligent. Witnessing the emotional distress in the eyes of those we love most, burdened with the knowledge that we no longer cherish our former selves, is a painful experience. In their eyes, we mattered most when we remained true to our core essence, the person they loved from the very beginning, unswayed by the world's influences. Family is a circle of care, and straying from it transforms us into strangers to those we hold dear.

The world we inhabit can be unforgiving, and the agony of realizing our diminished significance compared to our former selves can be overwhelming. In such moments, we reflect on our inner worth and contemplate who truly deserves the person we've become and the life we've chosen, seeking a deeper understanding.

You've been summoned into the life you're living now. The same reason that brought you on this journey of understanding might start to feel like your adversary. You'll be surprised that things won't make sense for you, and it might seem like you're against everything out there. The world will keep moving in its own direction, and often, you'll find yourself alone, trying to find your place to share your knowledge. If you fail, you might end up alone, especially in matters of love, where no one will care about you, who you are, or what you're doing.

Even though knowledge, life, and love have called you, the opposite of what you represent and the reasons behind your calling will keep you restless. You'll tirelessly fight to see your plans succeed. At times, you might envy what others are doing and wish you were part of it, becoming an enemy to your own ideals.

You can start anywhere you like, but often, these are situations young men and women go through when they have desires to stand out. Despite risking your life, you must be confident in your potential for success. You might wonder if you truly are wise or if your intelligence is genuine since your journey started with exposure to the global reality.

You might find yourself in a situation where you've given everything to an idea, and depending on how much you've given, there might be nothing left of you. When you dedicate your life to something, don't let the world change you. Remember, you're a unique individual capable of so much.

Never forget your true self; it's more important than the challenges you face. You could be a young person in a world that seems to have taken everything from you, reminiscing about who you used to be. It's all part of the path you've chosen, to work and live in harmony with your understanding, even though the road is filled with obstacles that obscure your true self.

Chapter Three

Goals So Distant

You need to do what you believe is necessary to become a part of life before you can make any progress. But who are you doing it for? Is it for me, the world, or perhaps everyone around you? Do we really care about the things we get involved in or the benefits we gain from our actions? Why do we continue to interact with the world all the time, and what are we trying to achieve with our ambitions? Who are we trying to please with all our efforts? It seems like it's taking too long, and it hasn't made the one person you wanted to be closer to happy.

All the patience and faith we have in our ideas, what is it meant for? Is it meant to make me happy, to make the world a better place, or just to bring me closer to the one I love and yearn to be with? Maybe we can find each other and spend time together, sharing the best moments of our lives and experiencing eternal joy. But for now, this competition with the whole world is leaving you feeling empty inside. There's no one to commit to, and you're spending too much time on your own, trying to get things right.

At the end of the day, who will benefit the most from all your efforts? It's that special person you're eagerly waiting for, the one you're trying to love and bring into your life in the distant future. The only person meant to be a part of your life forever. Maybe that person will find joy in the beauty you've worked so hard to create. But for now, everything around you is broken, and no one can come close to you or seem to care. You're just alone.

It often seems that what we do pleases people we don't really care about, while the one person you truly want to make happy remains elusive. You spend most of your time focusing on something that feels important, but in reality, you're missing the point with much of what you do, and it's even worse than expected as you continue to lose yourself.

We often find ourselves struggling to bring happiness to the people we intend to serve, and, in the process, we receive sympathy from those not directly involved in our mission. This predicament raises questions about its impact on us. It can divert our attention away from the present moment and lead us to seek meaning in the distant future. Yet, it's crucial to remember that happiness is a current concern; it's where we are right now that gives us purpose. However, when we embark on significant endeavors, we may lose ourselves in the process.

In pursuit of distant goals, we may endure present hardships, anticipating eventual rewards. So, how do we find solace in such a situation or come to terms with seemingly fruitless efforts? Although we may initially set our sights on a distant life, the challenge lies in nurturing an idea from its inception into a solid foundation that sustains us. Our desire for happiness, financial stability, or worldly influence is valid, but we must align these aspirations with a purpose that serves society's needs and our human essence.

This approach ensures that we don't exploit the world's kindness; instead, we must find a unique angle or subject to contribute meaningfully. Keep in mind that we aren't naturally equipped with this level of understanding; we are born with the right to work and earn a living without such complexities. It may not solely depend on your actions or how others perceive you; instead, it can revolve around your creation, which may take longer than expected to find its place in the universe.

This journey may create disparities between you and your peers, even those of similar age and life stages. Progress can be slow as you strive to develop a meaningful concept that resonates not only with you but also with humanity as a whole. It's about pursuing your passion, believing it will impact the world positively, and having faith in its eventual success. Nothing can thwart your goal except the passage of time, which may delay your attainment of a fulfilling life.

Putting so much on hold to focus on your future aspirations is no easy feat. Sacrificing the present can be painful and disheartening, as your efforts may not yield immediate results. Imagine living a life devoid of accomplishments despite your best attempts. We must continually set and achieve goals to gain a sense of self-worth before our physical capabilities wane, or we become emotionally drained and fatigued.

Living without earning something from life is nearly impossible, unless you've accumulated a substantial amount of resources to sustain yourself. When you rely solely on faith, your physical and emotional well-being can deteriorate over time because not everyone around us is prepared for the path we choose. You might be the only one meant for that particular journey, and you shouldn't try to hold people back or drag them along with you. Many people desire to rid themselves of such burdens in their lives; nobody wants to be pulled down with you.

As you progress, you'll come to realize that reaching your goal is a personal endeavor, driven by your own vision. You'll often find yourself facing tests of faith, and it's only when you feel the strain that you truly face a trial. To truly embody your beliefs, you must be tested on all fronts. Along the way, weariness and temptation may threaten to derail you, making you consider embracing your responsibilities just to make a living.

Your goals may seem distant, and happiness may still elude you as you yearn for it with all your heart. Your journey relies on faith, and your life hinges on hope, leaving you to wonder whom you can lean on. The present moment takes precedence above all else, as it is what we strive to live for. So, when you momentarily set aside your responsibilities to chase your dreams in the future, how do you cope with feeling disconnected from your humanity in the interim? Perhaps our longing to matter and be part of creation transcends all else, driving us to remain patient, regardless of the time it takes. What can we learn about the universe from this?

Devoting your entire understanding to a specific idea, one that means more to you than anything else, and clinging to it despite occasional setbacks, is a remarkable pursuit. It becomes inconsequential how you may feel left behind at times, as long as you ultimately achieve your goal. This way, you can spend the rest of your life with the pride of having mastered something that not only makes sense to you but also holds significance for the entire universe. Don't forget the importance of doing things correctly and precisely along the way.

Sometimes, it's important to live in the world you've built with your knowledge. You're eager to see it come to life, and a lot of your focus has been on that. However, things have changed now that you're striving for something more meaningful. Your path isn't as easy anymore because of your strong interest in creating something unique. In this new life you've chosen, your plans are set on distant horizons, which is unfortunate because it's happening at a time when you have pressing needs. When you were a child, you couldn't have imagined this, but now that you're here, at a point where things make sense, it's clear that your journey isn't the conventional way of being human.

From where you are now to your desired destination, it might take a considerable amount of time. You know it won't happen overnight; it'll take longer than you initially expected. However, when it finally comes to fruition, it will hold significant meaning for you, and it will bring clarity to your life that extends throughout the entire universe. You had the option to settle for anything, but circumstances led you to dedicate your entire knowledge to this unique path.

How often do you encounter people who are on a quest to discover their individual potential? In your physical circle, there are hardly any such individuals, making your journey even more challenging because you're not imitating anyone else. The idea you're pursuing is entirely your own. You might have thought of the world of human beings with special talents as a kind of imaginary realm, and now you must adapt it to become your reality.

This path you're pursuing was forged through your own understanding and knowledge. There may come a time when you feel like giving up because you're uncertain about where it's leading you. Another aspect that makes life somewhat challenging to find contentment in is the uncertainty of whether you truly influence success, wealth, or love. It might just be a great idea with no earning potential, and when you're deeply involved, it might not bring you any returns. So, where do you go to make a living and have a typical relationship? Your understanding of this all hinges on the same outcome, and that's what makes it complex.

As an individual, you possess everything that makes you who you are at this very moment. Your goals and objectives become clearer when you set specific timeframes for achieving them. Some goals are closer to reach than spending your entire life in pursuit of something unattainable. It's important to set goals that are achievable and easy to reach early in your journey. Sometimes, journeys take longer than expected, and you must maintain your faith and adapt to circumstances that may not align with your identity.

It's crucial to stay grounded in your knowledge and find contentment in the life you can currently only imagine. The duration it takes to accomplish something may not always matter; it's essential to discern between what you can control and what you can't. Some aspects of success may be beyond our influence, but we still desire to shape our futures. However, we often overlook the complexity involved in achieving success, as many obstacles can hinder our progress.

Love should not be underestimated. You can work diligently to nurture the tender aspects of our lives, seeking not just any love but a genuine, quality love. While money is a necessity, it only becomes a part of your success when you discipline yourself to incorporate it effectively. Though your journey may still be long, you can find contentment in your current state, acknowledging that some aspects of life are beyond your control, and much has already been bestowed upon humanity.

What enhances reliability is recognizing the individuals who have contributed value to the flow of creation throughout history. They form a cycle of experiences in the universe and have made it meaningful. This cycle encompasses knowledge from the beginning of time, passed down through the ages to the present, where we seek to partake in its treasures.

With the knowledge we possess, we have not accumulated much experience. We arrived on this journey with only ourselves and no one to lean on. At times, we may fail to perceive the absolute truth because we are confined to our individual perspectives. Consequently, we may find ourselves questioning our competence. It's not only intimidating for the world to embrace our ideas, but it's also daunting for others to place their trust in us. This distinction sets organizations apart from governments.

Initially, you may experience loneliness, but if you succeed, you will establish an organization with a robust foundation. You'll have effectively organized information until everything coherently falls into place. This is not about competition; rather, it's about striving to restore harmony in creation through your accumulated knowledge. On the contrary, individuals who serve the government receive what they need, leading to a stark contrast.

Understanding the reason for feeling left behind stems from the inherent disparities between the world outside and our lived experiences. It's crucial to remember that we do not serve the same entity. Sometimes, you might forget you are navigating this journey alone and start attributing your challenges to the universe.

These are aspects that one can overlook when confined to their own understanding. Failing to recognize your current position is a possibility, whether you are devoted to an organization or deeply committed to expanding your own knowledge. Therefore, it is essential to continuously self-reflect, assess your progress, and gain a clear perspective. Overindulgence in your creativity might blind you to the actual state of affairs, leading to a skewed perception.

Ultimately, we are responsible for ourselves, and the external world is drawn to us based on the value we offer or personify. Regardless of how others may influence your comprehension, your own worth is paramount. Occasionally, we place undue faith in others and overlook the fact that we are on distinct, independent journeys.

Embarking on a creative journey may seem simple in the beginning, but as you progress, you may encounter challenges in grasping the true essence of things until you achieve success. When we observe the world of creation from an external perspective, we find thriving businesses that have been established by individuals who dedicated relentless effort until they flourished.

Regardless of whether you inhabit a vast or a compact world, it's crucial not to overlook the importance of perceiving reality as it truly is. It's easy to fall into the trap of delusion, distorting your perception of the universe, ultimately deceiving yourself. Recognizing your place as an integral part of the broader context, even when it feels distant, is vital. At some point, we all adhere to our personal ideas, and this remains unchanged until you embrace a new perspective.

To integrate into the world that exists beyond, one that aligns with the reality you aim to manifest and the realm of creation in which we all participate, consider whose vision you align with before discovering your own path or establishing a meaningful life. Three distinct levels of creation beckon: comprehending the constructs of governance, aligning with the concepts of an established organization, or forging your unique path to success. Instead of lingering in contemplation, focus on genuine achievement through your distinctive thought process. This is how your knowledge should ultimately reward your endeavors.

Do not waver or offer minimal effort; immerse yourself entirely in your quest to comprehend life. It necessitates an abundance of energy so that everything starts to coalesce, especially as you encounter numerous obstacles that might attempt to drain your resolve and dismantle the mental creations you seek to nurture. Finding connection with all that exists is imperative, and if you succeed, your daily well-being will become remarkably productive and perpetually fulfilling.

Life often surprises us, and it may not unfold as we initially thought. You might gain insight sooner or perhaps realize things too late. Sometimes, you grasp the truth early on, but at times, understanding dawns only after time has passed. When you're out on your own and working for your organization, you may feel like the world cares for you, but in reality, there's little beyond your existence. What truly matters is the reality you create, where your knowledge paves the way for success. This is particularly crucial in the early stages of life.

If you aspire to develop your own ideas, it's essential to assess your position. You don't need to struggle due to a lack of understanding, especially given the unforgiving nature of the world we live in. Either you comprehend the choices we make or you don't; your life is in your hands for much of your journey. It's not that we neglect love at times, but rather that you must play your part to reach a point where everything starts to make sense. Seeking a fulfilling relationship where you know it isn't can lead to discontent, as can believing it serves a particular purpose when it doesn't.

The confusion we face along the way often arises from external factors influenced by our actions. While you may strive to understand life, much of it can still be perplexing. You can't expect love from someone you deliberately choose to be with, nor can you pay yourself money; these things come from external sources. Continuing on this path can lead to frustration, as human interactions, based on your comprehension, may hold you back.

Interactions with others, particularly in matters of love, require agreement and comfort in giving oneself to another. Money is also handled from this perspective, and it's crucial to thoroughly grasp these aspects of our lives, whether you have goals to achieve. Don't overlook these crucial facets, for they ultimately matter the most in the grand scheme of things.

People have different beliefs about life, which often leads to conflicts because of our varying perspectives. Many people will come and go in your life, but those who truly matter will stay. It's essential to try and understand others' points of view, as your perspective isn't the same for everyone. Changing someone's viewpoint can be challenging.

Failing to understand others can be problematic, as they bring valuable insights to the table. Money and love often come from interactions with people who see the world differently. If you can't agree, you'll keep searching for essential things you once had and wonder what's wrong with you.

Sometimes, you become part of the problem, making your life worse. When people with different views are involved, it's tough to assign blame. Are you the solution or part of the issue? Achieving results takes time and understanding.

Life won't suddenly improve; you'll encounter challenges you don't fully grasp. When you finally connect with life and reach your goals, you'll have put in a lot of effort. Until then, you're not exempt from working hard and striving for success, sticking to your own approach and doing whatever it takes to achieve your goals.

Why do things seem so far from who you are and what you know? What do you expect to experience? There's a lot to learn, and sometimes it can feel overwhelming. Life often demands responsibilities that you might not have been prepared for. Perhaps you can gain knowledge along the way, but what about those you have to deal with who haven't learned yet?

There are people, like a woman who hasn't discovered how to truly love and spends all her time neglecting her duties to care for someone. Or a man who lacks integrity when dealing with others, even though he plays an important role in bringing people together.

Maybe you just need to learn patience and adapt to various situations, which is a rare quality to find. We often pursue our desires vigorously but may not be as committed to other important aspects of life. You focus on making your ideas a reality, but are you equally focused on what truly matters, like love?

Are you merely talking about it without living it? These are two different things: wanting success through knowledge and actually achieving it, especially when it aligns with your financial goals. Everything should make sense, both internally and externally.

While seeking a meaningful relationship, you might not find one, even though your ideas suggested great things should come your way. You expected good returns, but now you feel let down. Can you remember your mindset before embarking on this journey for greater love? Why did you associate everything you do with true love? Why was building strong connections and making money such a central focus, even if it hasn't been as easy as you hoped? These are the questions to ponder.

You once had big dreams, hoping for a deep understanding of life. Your goal was to achieve excellence in all your desires, spend more time with your loved ones, and enjoy long-lasting love rather than constantly dealing with responsibilities. It's ironic how we often seek abundance but end up with scarcity. You may have faced moments of lack despite your needs.

Can you find peace when everything feels distant, love seems elusive, and money is scarce? You don't receive what you desire daily, and you yearn for it now to feel better about yourself. When is the right time if not today? Can circumstances allow us to make our dreams a reality where we are? Are you willing to sacrifice your vision to make it a reality sooner?

We may not know what the future holds, but we can be certain of our own ideas and endeavors. Whether we build on this foundation or keep things as they are, the important thing is that we've started. Even if it feels like a competition you must win, remember, you can't truly lose. You need to make a living; otherwise, it seems like there's no way to achieve your goals, leaving you with nothing.

You didn't think your ideas were solely for you, but now you're realizing they've become a competition you can't seem to win against yourself. If you don't follow the path your vision has laid out, you may feel like you've failed to fulfill your role as a member of society.

Could you take a leap of faith? There comes a time when you might not question why it's the right moment; you just need to keep in mind that serving others matters every single day. You must not forget this responsibility, as it's a crucial aspect of our journey. Sometimes, when we pursue everything without pause, we realize that not everything we accumulate truly counts. Nevertheless, it remains incredibly significant and is the very reason why we embarked on this path in the first place. Without this guiding purpose, our efforts would lack meaning, and the risks we take might not be worth it. Everything we do is built upon the foundation of our developed skills.

We engage in this endeavor to test our limits and explore the myriad directions where success may await. Ultimately, you must grasp that dedicating yourself to something meaningful in life always carries a degree of risk. You should always keep in mind that unforeseen obstacles can disrupt your plans. Therefore, we approach our pursuits with a solid foundation, ensuring that we don't lose our way. Think of it as a trial of your ideas for their reliability. If things don't unfold as expected, what would be your course of action?

As you progress, you may stumble upon a promising idea, yet you may face two pivotal factors that often shape the success of any endeavor: love and money. These elements aren't adversaries; instead, they are coveted rewards that crown our efforts. Achieving them becomes a personal aspiration. You strive to witness everything falling into place, and, at the end of the day, would it really hurt to surrender to circumstances in order to attain them?

Understanding that you might not change the entire world, would you still seek to make a positive impact, regardless of the outcomes? What conditions would make you feel comfortable? Can you commit yourself to something, secure in the knowledge that you won't be in a state of desperation for the rest of your life? You need a solution, and perhaps the key lies in establishing a strong foundation. Once that's in place, you can dedicate yourself to pursuing your desires with determination. It's akin to raising children from birth, nurturing them to become everything they can be, while you, as the parent, continue to live and do what you deem necessary.

Chapter Four

Good Intentions

Perhaps we should not always place the blame for a situation solely on women. Instead, we can approach it with reason and let our good judgment guide us. Women's rights, in some aspects, might involve granting them the freedom to not be burdened by knowledge and its consequences. They could enjoy the flexibility of life, always having the liberty to be free.

This was often the case in situations where men were compelled to delve deeply into the realm of creation. This compulsion led them to think beyond the ordinary and foster creativity. On the other hand, women were granted the freedom to live their lives without such pressures. Everything that was part of their lives was done with good intentions for them. This could certainly be one of the reasons why they are capable of love, even amidst the complexities that knowledge brings.

Women, like anyone else, can face the frustrations of life and relationships. At times, it's not just about finding someone to be with whenever you want or feel the need for love. It's about giving yourself to the right person who can offer you quality in every aspect. It's about knowing that this unique individual will never misuse your commitment and takes your presence seriously.

True love and happiness stem from finding someone who cares for the entirety of your being. So, if you're a woman who has engaged in groundbreaking endeavors, it can be quite challenging when it comes to love. If you don't succeed right from the start, it can feel like a battle against everything you're doing. It's evident that nothing truly wants to be fully controlled by humans if it possesses a life force; it strives to break free.

It becomes challenging to desire something from the universe without first mastering it or completing your ongoing projects. Things start making sense on the other side of life, where there's clarity in what we do. That's where one can find happiness and realize that life holds meaning. Then you might ask yourself, why? Why does love become the greatest sacrifice of all human qualities, especially when the outcome matters more than our current way of living?

Women's rights have always existed in various forms, especially when men struggled to grasp their responsibilities in our current world. It's not easy to establish a space for mutual love and understanding; people often stumble and fall when they attempt to stand strong in this modern age.

We all seek meaning in the world around us, exploring different paths taken by humanity. Sometimes, we come up empty-handed, except when we find ourselves lost within a particular way of doing things. In those moments, it's crucial to do everything possible to regain understanding, perhaps allowing us to rediscover love and bring life back into focus.

We are born with a certain level of understanding that defines our normality. If we stick to the familiar path, we continue to grow and develop as expected throughout life. However, what can be truly frustrating is when we encounter complex concepts in our creative journey, as we try to derive meaning from our own perspectives. Proceeding with uncertainty about our actions can profoundly impact everything we hold dear.

In the vast world around us, it's easy to feel lost sometimes. It's not that you don't know what you're doing; it might be because of the path you've chosen for your life. Sometimes, even in a well-established culture, what you're engaged in may not seem to fit in. Nobody seems interested, and you might even try bending the rules to get noticed. But how long can you keep that up?

It's tough when you can't be true to yourself, and living without what you desire most can be really hard. To reach your goals, you might have to make sacrifices, and going against the current lifestyle can be tough on your well-being. Love, on the other hand, is innocent. It doesn't oppose anything; it flows with creation and creativity, whether it's seen as good or bad, as long as it contributes to the world's progress.

Today, when we feel like we're missing true love and happiness, we sometimes blame women for being subjective and biased in their decisions and opinions. But true love doesn't have a specific season, place, or time. Many women have never questioned what might be missing in their lives.

Confusion often arises when men seek to understand themselves and the path of creation. Especially when they're on the journey of knowledge and creativity, trying to figure out who they are and how to improve.

Regardless of your intentions, it's worth asking if the world needs people like us—those seeking to understand life, valuing knowledge and creativity. Is there room for intelligence? Can you honestly say that your life serves a worthy purpose from beginning to end, and that everything you do justifies your way of living? It could be about where we stand in the grand scheme of creation and human history. The universe we live in has advanced so much that it might seem there's little left to develop beyond what's already been achieved.

You might find yourself pondering many questions, trying to figure out what's absent in the world, and if you were to develop a particular idea, would people appreciate it? Will people eagerly embrace your efforts, even if they take longer than expected? Could there be imitators, substitutes, or copycats that might burden you when you finally reach your destination, diminishing your significance? Given that people have options, something should justify the time you've devoted to crafting your ideas. Things should make sense in the end.

In the realm of creation, individuals have made sacrifices in such a manner that regardless of what the world seeks, it can continue to draw inspiration from those who have dedicated themselves to fostering positive change. They have wholeheartedly committed their lives to witnessing substantial greatness emerge, driven by good intentions.

This approach makes a lot of sense and validates the commitment of one's life. Others may possess talent, but lack the courage and discipline to give their all to their aspirations. Furthermore, in a world filled with innovation, can one genuinely carve out a niche and identify a compelling need? And if so, do they possess the necessary qualities to execute their vision successfully?

Suppose, hypothetically, one can still think creatively in this fast-paced and challenging world, and they manage to create something significant that fulfills a genuine demand. In that case, it becomes imperative to emphasize that by wholeheartedly dedicating oneself to the task, they not only transcend the limitations of their era but also become the most influential and trustworthy figure of their time. This can truly make a substantial difference and contribute to greatness.

So, how can you determine whether your idea will address a critical need or merely fill a void in global creation? A strong vision resides in a heart driven by good intentions, fueled by a genuine desire to assist humanity. It aligns with and gives purpose to your actions. This is the kind of conviction one should strive to embody when pursuing their goals.

While you may not initially find what you're searching for, if you persist and continue on your journey, you'll eventually reach a point where there's a need to fulfill, and you'll be recognized and appreciated for your efforts. This won't happen suddenly, but rather, it will emerge from your deepest desires. To succeed in this endeavor, it's important to be clear about your inventions and your intentions behind them. Can you identify your goals and objectives without being solely motivated by money? Can you remain dedicated to the end result, focusing on how it can positively impact the world?

It would be truly remarkable to pinpoint a genuine need that you can address, which will drive you to help others and keep your concept alive, regardless of the challenges life may throw your way. How can you be certain that your intentions remain pure, especially when the world becomes harsh and challenges your efforts? Is there a nagging doubt that seeks to undermine your commitment to doing what is right, given the circumstances you've faced along the way?

For some individuals, comprehending this path of creation might be difficult, as they may not have experienced the truth or genuine love. Yet, deep down, you originally aimed to do good, but circumstances may have shifted your ultimate purpose, leading you astray. Some may even find themselves stuck in a pattern of dishonesty, despite their initial good intentions. It can be challenging to maintain honesty and goodness in a world that often presents difficulties from that perspective. Nevertheless, upholding these values is crucial, as developing a negative attitude may come at the cost of your own well-being. Your life is always on the line, no matter the circumstances.

Firstly, let's talk about the importance of having a kind heart. It's crucial if you want to make a big impact. Always remember why you wanted to help people and don't lose sight of that. This defines who you are, even when things get tough. Don't let anger at the world or others take away your purpose. Some things can be hard to understand, but that's just the way the world is sometimes.

Now, let's reflect on two things: sticking to the truth and having the flexibility to use your knowledge. But for you, honesty has always been your guiding principle, something deeper than what most people can grasp. No matter how frustrating the world can be, you've known that your life is at stake. So, you may need to be careful about what you get involved in, especially when you're working on something. Sometimes, challenges can push you in unexpected directions.

One thing that can lead to depression is pursuing a path that doesn't exist. The world may acknowledge your discovery, but it may have already moved forward, or you might create something new that humanity can live without. Even if your ideas aren't entirely novel, they may offer a competitive advantage, and you hope people will see that. Sometimes, people need time to adapt to change, and their reactions show how hard it can be to adjust quickly.

Every new invention or idea needs time to catch people's attention. Once that happens, the next challenge is to win their loyalty. People are accustomed to using existing services, so gaining their trust for something new can be tricky. They may not be ready to change their habits. The way things are can be frustrating, especially when it feels like the world isn't embracing your ideas. However, sometimes it's just a matter of giving them a chance to see the value.

Can the future make up for what you've been through? Perhaps someone will come into your life and help you forget the loneliness, rejection, frustration, and confusion you've faced. Love has the power to heal and make you more accepting of the challenges you've encountered while trying to find your place in the world.

When you open your heart to someone special, they can help you forgive the world for necessary but difficult decisions made along the way. Sometimes, pursuing a long-term goal means putting your life on hold while the rest of the world continues. But remember, nothing lasts forever.

Life can throw situations at you that make you doubt your path and the reasons you started a particular project. It's easy to lose sight of your initial intention, which was likely to make a positive impact on people's lives. Many individuals who began their journey focused on projects or businesses found themselves changed by the situations they encountered while navigating this complex world.

Over time, it's easy to lose sight of who you are, what drives your ambitions, and what you truly desire. However, despite the challenges, remember that your initial intention was to make a difference in the lives of others.

Many people could have had better lives, but they faced pressure they couldn't handle. This pressure made them lose sight of their self-worth. It's important not to let difficult situations change who you are or make you choose a path you didn't want.

Don't allow anything to steal your happiness. Love can bring happiness, so don't give up on yourself easily. People can't adjust to new situations overnight. It takes time to discover your true self and connect with life. Even if you come from a tough background, you can succeed if you stay focused on your goals.

Remember, success often comes with sacrifices and challenges, but it also brings rewards. It's crucial to stick to your goals no matter how tough things get. Understanding love is essential before letting anger take over. If you don't know how to care, you won't make a positive impact on others.

Imagine facing the toughest situations and feeling like you're losing your goodness. You can't go back to who you once were. Something might have changed in you, and you may have gained power but lost your compassion. You start fighting against everything in your path, feeling like the world is against you. This can be frustrating when all you need is motivation for your projects.

What if you wanted to make the world different than it used to be? Maybe you thought something was wrong with it. So, you decided to take a personal responsibility and said, "I'll fix this, no matter what it takes." But when everything seemed to go against what you understood, it became personal. You were willing to give everything you had to make a difference, but when things got tough, you chose a path you hadn't originally intended.

Does this world deserve punishment for how it's changed or for failing to grasp the truth of its current state? Where should we draw the line and do what's right? Is the authority we possess enough to judge this universe if it's become something unexpected? Can we truly blame someone for how things turned out? Do we penalize people by becoming something we didn't intend to be, or by creating something that will disrupt their lives in response to what they've done to ours?

Where is the person who once knew and understood their purpose well, the one who wanted to heal others and make a meaningful impact in this lifetime? Certain situations we encounter along the way can alter one's life if they aren't prepared to stay disciplined. Love is what truly hurts; not having someone to care for you can shatter a human heart, making it nearly impossible to mend. It brings happiness to return to a loved one, but what if that's been taken away, leaving you without anyone to care for?

The frustrations, confusion, and challenges of life that we face on our journey can become overwhelming if we don't share them with others. How can you just move on from everything? Most of it doesn't make sense because it's something you didn't know or understand, and it needed to be mastered for you to find contentment in your actions and in the creation around you.

Love is a feeling we should always seek. It helps us forget daily difficulties. But when life's pressures keep growing, it can weaken us. We might lose sight of our daily goals. Life requires preparation. When you focus on a task, it can become challenging. But what if you could push aside distractions and stay on track? Even when the path seems unclear, don't look back. Your aim is to help people through your understanding, so keep going.

Remember, you're not a harmful person, and don't let challenges make you doubt yourself. Live well, be ready for anything. You never know who might use your ideas or products. Always remember that impatience can lead to negative consequences and exploitation.

When life gets tough during your quest for understanding, you'll encounter tests of patience. People may try to mold you into what they want, but if you aspire to greatness, you can choose your own path. See your job as one of your responsibilities, and approach it with dignity and respect.

We live in a time where external forces can influence us, but is that a good thing? Life often presents challenges. If you've complained about imperfections, now you have a chance to make a difference, instead of arguing from a distance.

When you get the opportunity to do what you believe is right, does it matter what you've been through to reach that point where you achieve your best in whatever you aim to be? Yes, anger can exist, but it's important not to let it control you. Instead, understand that over time, you can become the person you aspire to be. Many times, the situations you go through can lead you to realize your dreams. However, if you don't overcome these challenges, you may become a victim of your current circumstances and its disappointments.

Many things will come and go, but what truly matters is the person you were at the beginning. Let that person continue to exist and experience their own reality. Allow it to shape your spirituality and motivate you in your work, guiding you to stick to your original plans.

Having good intentions means you'll do things the right way, even if you've faced disappointments. Live to ensure that the person who emerges into the light is the one you were meant to be. In a world where you interact with others, don't let anyone take advantage of you. Strive to achieve greatness in this vast reality.

Life should reflect the choices you've made for yourself. Don't let unforeseen circumstances make your goals seem impossible, causing you to lose sight of who you are. Each time you overcome life's challenges, you move closer to your desires. To reach your ambitions and truly own your destiny, you may need to go through various stages of your journey. This is how you'll ultimately achieve your goals and aspirations.

Remember that what you do can be taken away from you, but it only truly becomes yours when you reach the end of your journey. Avoid self-destructive behavior due to fear of the outcome of your actions. Commit to seeing through what you've started and discover whether the world is truly against you or if it's just the path you've been traveling.

Chapter Five

In my head

Individualism, which we often encounter on our journey towards innovation and understanding, resides within the depths of one's intellectual capacity. It appears that the world grapples with attaining clarity and precision regarding why many struggle to find happiness. This, in turn, affects how we perceive someone's desire to excel and be understood. Ultimately, it may become the most profound truth in human development, evident in our ability to create and adapt to new ideas when intelligence and creative thinking are successfully harnessed.

Certain things that might have seemed ordinary or logical often circle back to the question of an individual's capabilities and knowledge. One's abilities must be sufficient to grant them freedom, for breaking through the barriers of knowledge lays the foundation for life itself. However, the dilemma lies in the process of comprehending and shaping ourselves, which may inadvertently lead to isolation more often than necessary. What requires understanding is the significance of invention within society. Regrettably, due to a lack of insight, we have failed to grasp these concepts effectively, allowing it to interfere with our perception of one's thirst for knowledge.

Consider this: What if, as a society, we have overlooked other crucial subjects that profoundly impact our lives and existence? These subjects could have yielded immediate results if we had only understood ourselves better. Yet, due to our lack of clarity on certain matters, we have often underestimated their seriousness, and it has consequently influenced our daily lives significantly.

As a result, we frequently find ourselves confronted by inexplicable circumstances that demand the development of unique skills to thrive amidst these challenges. We are compelled to comprehend matters that many find disconcerting, causing them to feel subjected to life's unpredictable qualities and pushing them beyond conventional circumstances. Although the overarching theme is the differentiation of our participation, we must each find our own path. But how can we accomplish this when so many external factors profoundly impact our lives? Nevertheless, we bear the responsibility of discovering our unique selves and cultivating distinctive concepts that set us apart from others and the world's prior experiences.

On our journey to find the life we desire, we encountered some strange things. Sometimes, it's okay to be alone because there's a need for goodness and discipline, as we wait for the right time to meet a worthy partner. But if we look closely, we realize that the very ideas we aim to master have trapped us. Could it be that as we try to follow our own paths and discover the world, we haven't found success or happiness because we've let ourselves down?

Have our journeys taken longer than they should have? Every time we tried to reinvent ourselves, it seems we couldn't find the solution. Our ultimate goal has always been a normal life, but our individual quests to define ourselves differently have become too challenging.

Regardless of the difficulty, these ideas stem from our desire for greatness. However, we mustn't let this purpose overshadow our search for true love. Ultimately, the world can't provide solutions for individuals when it comes to love. We find our own happiness by understanding ourselves. Embracing individualism doesn't mean isolating oneself. By dedicating ourselves to our pursuits, we create the perfect partner who aligns with our goals.

So, if we allow discipline to guide our work, we can still express our unique concepts without sacrificing love. We must remember that caring for someone is a fundamental human need, independent of our stage of personal development. We all seek that special person to care for, which is a common aspect of our humanity. The rest is shaped by our pursuit of greatness.

As we progress, we become intellectuals, contemplating issues of higher intelligence relevant to our creative endeavors. This influences how we operate and how others perceive us. You can consider love from two perspectives: through creative involvement or in a more conventional life. You'll realize that a conventional path offers flexibility, while creativity demands discipline for a harmonious relationship with the world.

When life's progress seems elusive, reflect on what might be going wrong. Even without external influences, everything begins with us. Ask yourself how you're perceived by the world. Are you living in a way that aligns with how you want to be known? Avoid conflicting these life concepts.

How does someone from outside our universe perceive the way we do things? We all have desires, but do we possess the willpower that truly drives us toward our goals? What's most significant is how our actions reflect the dignity of the world we engage with, especially when one part of us is fully committed while another part struggles to align. When we dedicate ourselves to a specific idea, we often face scrutiny from everything around us. People wonder about our intentions, our motivations, and whether we engage in pursuits for a specific purpose or merely to fulfill personal needs. If given the chance to become someone else, would we consider it to escape compromises on our desired path?

In my mind, a constant battle ensued, driven by my deepest ambitions, yet I couldn't ignore the world beyond. Nevertheless, I remained deeply committed to my personal will. In matters of love, I told myself that divine blessings would come at the right time, and anyone entering my life would be exceptionally special, held close to my heart. At times, I encountered numerous voices attempting to reshape my thoughts, questioning my life choices, pushing me beyond conventional expectations. I found reasons to focus on my goals, even when my motivation waned.

For those navigating their own understanding, the path may seem challenging to reach. One can opt for the easier way out or stay true to their aspirations, even if it means enduring moments of vulnerability due to overwhelming circumstances. Amidst the internal chaos, we must remember that we are not celestial beings; we are part of this world, shaping our decisions based on societal influences. Despite desiring the same things as everyone else, our unique experiences lead us down unfamiliar roads.

Understanding this world can bring shame. Each time our motives are questioned, we yearn to explain and justify ourselves for better comprehension and forgiveness. These are struggles we all encounter as we immerse ourselves in our chosen pursuits. The integrity of being content where we are is often challenged, forcing us to live in harmony with our true values. The present reflects the culmination of our inner journey, shaping our lives outwardly.

It is very important to create ample opportunities for yourself to find someone to love and commit to. However, as you immerse yourself daily in creative work, you may find it challenging to make time for true love. Consequently, you might have missed out on the chance to love that special person in your life, and this could explain the loneliness you feel within yourself. One aspect of your life can influence another, and all your various commitments have led to situations where you are often alone and very lonely. While you are eager to address this, your ambitions also require your attention. You realize that you've embarked on a significant journey by applying your knowledge, and now your success depends on it.

In a world without competition for your endeavors, you might have had more success. However, given that you've recently discovered an idea that already exists elsewhere, it has become difficult to make meaningful progress. While you have the potential to contribute to improving human lives, competing with existing solutions complicates matters and affects what you hold dear.

This struggle challenges everything you engage in, and you may find yourself caught up in a life you didn't anticipate. Perhaps you initially sought a better way of living, and when circumstances seemed insurmountable, you took it upon yourself to pursue your desires. It could have been a journey where you questioned the purpose of your current path and decided to make a change for the better.

The impact this path can have on your well-being is unpredictable. You may feel trapped and judged by circumstances, questioning your origins. Ultimately, the destination is more important than the route, but how long will it take for everything to make sense? Especially now, as you navigate this journey, you'll not only learn to do good things but also become entangled in both positive and negative actions. In the end, you may find it necessary to isolate yourself from the world's distractions, focusing solely on what demands your attention, thereby enhancing the quality of your work.

Learning inappropriate behaviors doesn't just harm your projects and goals. It can also leave a gap in human society, making people look for alternatives to what you've created. If you build something meant for specific people but not everyone, many will be dissatisfied with your invention. People will seek solutions for equal opportunities so that everyone can benefit.

What can be truly concerning about your creation is that others may try to exploit it. When there's room for manipulation within your creation, some will try to exploit it, while others are left out. Those who feel ignored may start inventing strategies to address their needs, and someone will eventually succeed.

Regardless of the challenges along the way, you must strive for a solution that benefits everyone. While it can be disheartening to ignore the world's current issues and focus solely on your own goals, you must persevere. Our reality allows you to define yourself or be shaped by external influences. Knowledge is transparent and helps clarify your objectives, guiding you toward your goals.

Sometimes, you might wonder if love could have made a difference or if seeking knowledge has altered your path. No idea is born complete; many require nurturing to make sense. Along the journey, temptations abound. However, remember to stay true to your path and not involve yourself in everything, as it may require sacrifices to remain authentic to yourself.

You should cherish the things that are close to your heart, even when you don't have all the answers right from the start, and even when many obstacles try to hold you back. Only when you bring your full passion into creating something, will things start to make sense to you at some point. However, it can be frustrating and confusing at times, as if you've dedicated yourself to a complete mystery. But remember, you'll discover your true self along the way because you matter just as much, if not more, than anything else out there. To succeed, you must learn to observe things and not worry too much, even if things aren't going exactly as you'd like right now.

Yes, the path you've chosen may not have all the answers to life's questions, but one positive aspect is that it's driven by the desire to make the world a better place. Even when you reach the end, let your motivation continue to be about doing things correctly and with precision. By being committed to creating well-being, you may not win every time, but if you ever fall short of achieving what you desire, your intentions will always be something to cherish.

Though you may not know when you'll reach your destination, it's important to maintain discipline in your thoughts and actions. As you journey toward your goals, many things may not turn out as bad as you fear, and this kind of behavior will allow you to savor some moments in life. So, keep moving forward without regrets, understanding that your knowledge is contributing to quality, even if it feels like things are taking longer than expected. Value every step of your journey because greatness lies along the entire path.

Finding value in an idea isn't always easy; it becomes a reality when you appreciate the person you've become. Keep going, knowing that success is never guaranteed in our endeavors, but with determination, it can be greatly esteemed. Regardless of the outcome, understand that what you are on the inside is the key factor, and it can either lead to a better place or lead to destruction.

You may not feel like you're on the right path forever, but there's greatness within you waiting to be discovered. Sometimes, your goals aren't solely shaped by your own desires; they can also be influenced by the values you hold dear. To achieve your purpose, you need to fuel it with your inner passion for life. Without that burning desire to stand out, you won't be able to seize opportunities or reach the goals you've set for yourself. Remember that everything around us is a result of human ingenuity. People create things to benefit from their own inventions. So, hold onto your unique ideas and live with dignity in pursuit of them.

Your aspirations could encompass anything you truly want to achieve, representing the freedom of your authentic self or fostering understanding. Let your motivations be rooted in doing good, not just for yourself but for the world at large. The intensity of your desire to attain something can be matched by the discipline required to bring it into your life. Achieving your goals often means navigating through chaos with the driving force of your passion.

Rarely does everything fall into place right from the beginning or simply by thinking about your goals. Great accomplishments often emerge from situations we can't fully comprehend at the outset. So, once you muster the courage to embark on a new idea, don't look back. Life may teach you that some things take longer than expected, but persevere to attract the outcomes you dream of.

As you approach a breakthrough, you'll realize your pivotal role in your journey to success. Much of what you've achieved comes from your own beliefs and efforts, not from external influences. Failing to conduct yourself with integrity can lead to dependency on others, but aligning with your objectives is the path to self-reliance and success. Remember, you don't need others to validate your journey. You are enough for the life you've chosen.

When you expand your horizons, you may find that the roles others once played in your life fade away, and you embark on a solo journey. It's easy to doubt your abilities, but you possess everything necessary to unlock the doors that have been closed in your life. Even in moments of loss, resilience emerges from within.

People are essential, especially when it comes to motivation. However, it's important not to rely solely on others. When you do, your own well-being becomes less important, and it's like a part of you has faded away. Success depends on your own understanding, and it requires your knowledge, strength, and intelligence to create a fulfilling life. Without realizing this, you're not on the right path.

It may seem like you're doing someone a favor by living the life you're leading, but you're actually not. You're being unkind to yourself by holding back your potential for greatness. You could have been living life on your terms, but if an opportunity for change presents itself, seize it. Even if you don't immediately see the way forward, the key is to embrace personal growth. You're progressing toward your desired destination.

As you continue along your chosen path, you're gradually shaping yourself to reach the goals you set out to achieve early in life. Along the way, you'll encounter challenges that may leave you wondering why you're in such situations. These moments serve as reminders of the reality people face and why you engage in your chosen pursuits. Regardless of how tough things get, remember your initial motivation. The outcome you desire remains within you, and as you progress, things will start to make sense if you stick to the path of discipline that leads to success.

You must become your own source of strength and motivation. If you're not there yet, seek something that ignites love and confidence within you. You'll realize that you're always the best choice for what you aspire to be, no matter your goals. For any purpose you pursue, nobody can deny your vision becoming a reality, as long as you put in the necessary effort and endure the challenges that test your patience along the way.

If you can endure and face whatever challenges arise on your journey, you'll grow stronger as you progress. Having love or someone dear in your heart can greatly improve your experience because it provides solace when the world throws obstacles your way. All you require is courage to sustain you; the rest will become pleasurable. How can you handle setbacks and disappointments without motivation to persevere? Pride arises from hard work and pursuing your beliefs, which becomes a crucial part of your goals if you don't allow distractions along your path.

The key is to stay resolute and carry your objectives through to the end. While some may question your goals, you must have a clear vision of what you hope to achieve and gain. Not everything will be enjoyable. This mindset helps you confront a world that consistently tries to hold you back. It's essential to ensure your dreams aren't just fantasies.

Even when things aren't as easy as you'd like, convince yourself of the reality you're striving for. Otherwise, doubts will cloud your mind amidst daily distractions that aren't aligned with your goals. So, stand firm and confidently pursue what you know, striving for excellence. Achieving this in our fast-paced, modern world isn't simple. We've entered an era where the universe appears self-sufficient, leaving few gaps to fill.

Outside, there's little that requires immediate attention because people's needs are met in various ways. What remains unfulfilled won't be significant. To address such situations, serious specialization becomes necessary. Without dedication, you risk losing yourself to something trivial, eventually questioning your identity.

It's curious how the journey of an innovator, who has striven to enhance the world, leads to divergence and separation. You realize the universe no longer requires the same contributions you've offered throughout your journey. It hungers for fresh perspectives and specialization in different realms of innovation.

The world we live in today has changed a lot. It requires someone who doesn't just test it briefly and disappear but instead, travels alongside it, exploring new opportunities and discoveries in our modern society. To reach this level of understanding, one must go through many experiences with dedication and possess a way of life that sets them apart from others. Many may try to take advantage of various situations, but only those who are genuine in their creations will endure.

You need to possess a way of life that differs from what most people have seen before. Strive to break free from conventional norms and venture in a new direction where your unique talents shine. Work diligently, starting from being unknown and unimportant to becoming an integral part of people's lives. Apply the principles of success consistently, and don't be discouraged by the complexities of life or the time it takes for dreams to materialize.

Don't confine yourself to preconceived notions. Go beyond the ordinary and discover uncharted territories. Embrace your uniqueness and kindness, which will ultimately lead to your distinctiveness. Every journey holds something valuable at its end, and even the most brilliant minds will appreciate your different approach. You work hard to stand out from the crowd, and it's gratifying to be given an opportunity when many aspire to rule the world by being everything to everyone.

Pay attention to every detail, for when you can't be everything, rejecting certain things can lead to lasting pain. Completing a project doesn't require an eternity; it demands courage and motivation to reach your desired destination and achieve the success you've always wanted. The fundamental question you should seek to answer as you venture out is whether you are making a difference, as that should be your foremost priority.

As life unfolds, it will test your true intentions, revealing whether you genuinely aim to make a positive impact. If your core motivation is indeed to create change, then always carry the notion of lending a helping hand wherever it's needed. You must never entertain the thought of using your presence to harm others, for the world won't let you escape consequences. On the other hand, if your mission is to achieve greatness, you'll find lasting happiness.

Life, undoubtedly, demands its toll, but it should never extract a cost from humanity. Strive to earn the world's admiration by offering your contributions selflessly. This is how you'll derive joy from your commitment to creativity.

As you progress and grow stronger, ensure that your work mirrors your inner passion. Identify those moments when you've made a difference, especially when you've aided people in dire need. It contradicts the very essence of innovation when individuals enter the arena driven solely by financial gain. While profit has its place, it should always be tied to a clear purpose that has been fulfilled.

No amount of money can truly outweigh the value of meaningful work, unless, of course, a crime has been committed. In such cases, the scales may tip unfavorably. Remember, people are willing to give their all when their lives are held in high regard. Our well-being outweighs our possessions.

Nonetheless, it's clear that people are likely to resist when their very existence is threatened, especially in cases where they perceive a threat to their well-being.

Most people believe in contributing to their lives, and it feels wonderful when you can save yourself. As we approach the end, we realize that it's more meaningful to bring something valuable to others, even if it's not about healing. It could be anything that shows care. Ultimately, it should address the eternal question that resides within everyone: What is my purpose in life?

You put in a lot of effort to reach a point where you're not just taking from others but also ready to provide for their needs and well-being. This is what truly makes a difference. If you can answer this question, then you've reached a place where people are willing to give in return for what they desire.

The journey may have been challenging, but when you reach this point, happiness floods in because all your efforts start to matter. You also find healing in the realization that you've made a significant impact with your knowledge, and the world will hold you in high regard for it. Knowing that you've come a long way with self-reliance and belief in your actions, you truly become a fulfilled individual.

Chapter Six

See Through Obstacles

You might say that a significant source of confusion arises from individuals' choices regarding their mode of engagement. Each voyage presents its own set of trials and tribulations, but occasionally, you might find yourself pondering whether you could have navigated such circumstances more effectively had you not adopted your initial outlook on life. Nonetheless, now that you've opted to confront reality through a different lens, you can genuinely introspect. What are the challenges that demand your unwavering attention, which ones can be skirted, and which remain impossible to avert your gaze from?

There are certain things that are specially designed for a particular purpose, and these things are a crucial part of your journey. They mainly focus on helping you progress towards the place you want to reach. They guide you on how to move more effectively in the direction of the life you've chosen. These things cannot be overlooked, as they form the path of the learning process. Going through them enables you to come nearer to your goal.

There are certain challenges that you might face, and these challenges can be quite painful emotionally. However, it's important to recognize that these challenges aren't necessarily related to your current actions or choices. Whether you find yourself stuck in these challenges or manage to overcome them, they won't have a lasting impact on your overall life journey. If you can embrace whatever difficulties are affecting your life, your daily well-being will continue to improve. When you encounter these types of problems, you may often ponder their origins and how you found yourself in such a situation.

Challenges might arise from various aspects of your life. There are diverse kinds of problems that people may encounter, such as feeling left behind in many areas or experiencing difficulties in matters of the heart. These issues can truly burden an individual as they strive to gain a better understanding of themselves. When relationships lose their sense of purpose because you've decided to concentrate on what currently demands your attention, motivation may wane.

Sometimes, there are moments when you find yourself in a bit of a dilemma. You're torn between focusing on your own life and making space for relationships, which are undeniably significant. But here's a thought: by achieving your goals and aspirations, you might pave the way to eventually connect with someone who can offer you all the love and fulfillment you truly merit. Rather than neglecting your genuine desires and getting trapped in total obscurity, where there's no room to pursue your heart's deepest passions and essential actions in this journey of existence.

This unique opportunity before you is truly a rare gem. While human connections are an essential part of our existence, it is paramount to align your actions with the desires of your heart. Embracing love is crucial, but it's equally important to explore other facets of life, regardless of how your choices might influence your relationships. Keep in mind that any setbacks encountered in your current endeavor could potentially have long-lasting repercussions in your journey through life.

If you truly desire success in your endeavors, you may find it beneficial to broaden your perspective beyond your current circumstances. Although we all yearn for love, taking the time to navigate through this experience can bring greater clarity and understanding. Love holds immense significance, standing tall as the utmost essential aspect of our lives, and you may never encounter anything as vital. The only instance where it faces a challenge is when an individual wholeheartedly commits to a specific project, one that will ultimately come to symbolize their entire life's purpose and principles.

It might not always be a choice you make or something you decide to ignore.

Sometimes, it can turn into a duty that you must embrace, and you can approach it with care and affection, and everything will be fine. This responsibility may just be one of the most significant aspects of your entire life that should not be underestimated. Instead, it should be a commitment undertaken with a deep understanding and unwavering determination.

Love is not supposed to frighten us; instead, it's meant to accompany us as we grow and develop. When you strive to make a living in this world, you become more receptive to meaningful relationships. However, at this moment, as you've taken on one of life's greatest challenges and gained a deeper understanding, you might find it necessary to commit more of your time and energy to your pursuits, ensuring that you have ample opportunities to achieve your desires.

I have always desired to gain a clear understanding of things. Is it possible that the obligations we assume in life might snatch away the precious moments we should be devoting to love? Could it be that the scant opportunities we possess get consumed? There might come a time when you find it necessary to allocate more time for your own well-being, depending on your emotional state. If it feels like there's nothing more valuable than your quest to comprehend this world, then you might be willing to make whatever sacrifices are required, no matter the cost.

Isn't it true that sometimes you might be focusing so much on your future that you forget to enjoy your present? This is because your current situation plays a significant role in determining your future prospects. Some individuals find greater reasons to cherish their present moments than to solely fixate on what lies ahead. Disregarding this fact could be considered quite unwise.

You don't always require a vast fortune to capture someone's heart. Instead, you can invest extra care and affection, delve into profound love, and ultimately conquer the heart of your most cherished person. Future happiness isn't guaranteed, but if you appreciate the value of the present moment, strive to dedicate yourself and persist in pursuing what you deem essential for success. You wouldn't wish to carry a lifelong burden of regret, would you? Should we relinquish our current possessions in pursuit of something novel, or should we seek a path to reconcile with the unattainable?

Being cherished by someone who currently holds immense significance in your life is something that should not be underestimated or disregarded for any reason. It constitutes the most crucial aspect of existence. These are the aspirations we aimed to achieve, though perhaps the path we envisioned did not necessarily facilitate an easier means for one to possess all that is essential for happiness in their present circumstances. Consequently, the path you have selected now opens the door to numerous opportunities and makes everything achievable once more, regardless of the potential toll on your happiness. Once your work is satisfactorily completed, no obstacle can hinder your progress, and your identity as a human being is defined by your well-established values.

If you truly cherish something or love it wholeheartedly, life shouldn't be the sole obstacle preventing you from reaching your most profound desires and denying you the right to happiness. If you find contentment in your current circumstances, believing that the world has generously bestowed upon you all you need to thrive, then you can pause your journey and start caring for the abundant blessings bestowed upon you.

We are constantly pursuing ambitious projects in order to enhance our worth. Our objective is to attain a level of accomplishment that could potentially grant us access to opportunities beyond our wildest aspirations. It's important to recognize that challenging circumstances can occasionally obstruct our view of the path ahead, potentially constraining our ability to appreciate both our current possessions and our true potential.

You find yourself in your current place, content with your current circumstances, even though you sense that if you were to strive for it, you might attain a sense of authenticity. How can you let go of the idea that holds you back and embrace a deeper understanding of your true self? How can you validate the life you lead if you've never truly been satisfied with your present situation, despite your extensive knowledge of the world around you?

Do people around you realize the extent to which you've diminished the worth of what you perceive, and the desire to witness something superior and more fulfilling than your current situation? Everything ultimately boils down to either life or love; you may find dissatisfaction in one or both, with your career often being the most crucial aspect. If your career doesn't bring you happiness or help you attain your life goals, especially if achieving those goals would be immensely significant to you, then it might be time to advance beyond your current level of knowledge and understanding.

When it comes to love, if you don't have it, you might want to seek it out on your own terms. And if life hasn't given you much to be happy about, and you feel like it's better to have a purpose, then you can pursue it. The point is, sometimes when we're young, our inner drive pushes us to succeed in both our work and relationships. But if you've lost sight of your worth, now it's up to you to take control of your life and put in the effort to attain your goals.

Understanding oneself isn't always easy, but it's a vital part of being human. You possess a deep inner connection to your true self, though sometimes it's challenging to access. Perhaps you're currently lacking the motivation to explore this aspect of yourself. When you feel like things aren't going well, it could be because you yearn for a sense of purpose but haven't yet found the right time and place. You might still feel trapped, like a caterpillar in a cocoon, afraid of the vibrant, victorious person you could become when you embrace your inner self.

If you can break free from self-limiting thoughts and truly immerse yourself in the world, embracing the wonder of existence like a child, you'll discover that nothing is beyond your reach. So, as you stand there, don't become a person devoid of desires that remain unfulfilled, yet you yearn for them with all your heart. Instead, embark on a journey to discover your true self, your deepest passions in life, and seize the beauty within them. This pursuit will not only guide you towards a fulfilling career within this vast world but also grant you the love you need in this ever-changing reality. It clarifies your values and fosters robust self-esteem for individuals who seek quality in their lives.

As an individual, you are aware of your heart's deepest desires and what you believe you rightfully merit, even though there are occasions when external factors hinder us from achieving our utmost capabilities. Therefore, if you find yourself unable to attain the relationship you are absolutely convinced you deserve above all else, how will you respond? Considering that there are circumstances you cannot simply accept and others you cannot imagine living without, it is essential to begin examining the legitimacy of the life you are currently leading.

Consider whether you genuinely merit that extraordinary individual who holds immense significance in your life. Is there an available space, a welcoming spot for this remarkable person to enter your world? While you may be aware of your worthiness, do you possess the necessary resources to attain what you rightly deserve? Can you take control of your life, even though numerous obstacles may attempt to obstruct your path? Nevertheless, should you approach this endeavor with diligence and an unwavering desire for your true self, there is no way you will not succeed in finding a means to attain it.

What is the most effective way for us to achieve our desires? Should we simply move toward our goals, rise, step outside, and seize them with determination? You are aware that your life might have been quite distant from your aspirations. However, by following this path, you will attain a plethora of opportunities. Many others may have faced setbacks on their journey to their desired destination, but you will distinguish yourself and succeed.

Sometimes, we hold ourselves back because of a mindset that limits us. This mindset often stems from not having something we take pride in. However, when you have a goal or a significant achievement, you start to understand that what you're searching for is your true self. It's the pride in our identity that saves our spirit and directs our energy towards the right path. You can't stay lost forever; you keep moving through the process of awakening your spirit and soul, where you gain control and display your inner strength.

You start to face situations with your level of understanding, which is what you're trying to use to draw the world's attention. In doing so, you create a connection point where you can effectively handle these situations. Our universe expands as we broaden our perspective. At each stage of life, we discover our true value. Now, think about a scenario where you haven't accomplished anything significant. In such a case, you may not receive as much from this wonderful creation; your potential is limited by the bounds of creation itself.

So, besides that, working towards something you know will increase your chances of living a fulfilling life with all the rewards you deserve. Just imagine if you accomplish something that nobody in the world ever expected someone to achieve. This would give you a significant advantage in receiving love and recognition during your lifetime. Now that you understand we have to pick ourselves up on our journey to success. This is only possible if you avoid burdening yourself with things that you know do not require your love and attention. You need to exert effort to build your own dreams, goals, and vision, or anything that offers you the opportunity to attain a deep level of understanding and lead an exceptional life.

Don't be scared by the complex ideas you think about when you're far away from them. Even though things might seem hard to grasp, it's only because you haven't gotten into them yet. If you get ready to work diligently, you might discover that you actually understand more than you could ever imagine from an outsider's perspective. Remember, you can't know everything from just looking in from the outside.

The key idea is to start in a good and peaceful manner. This is especially important as you embark on the journey of life. When you begin with a simple understanding of reality and continue to evolve in that direction, you may not see immediate results in your pursuit of personal well-being. However, as time progresses, you will come to appreciate the valuable lessons you acquire along the way. It's important to understand that the path we embark upon in life is a continuous source of learning, and one should never assume that they have already learned everything they need to know.

Misunderstandings we face as we journey through life are like puzzles for our minds to solve. They challenge us to gain a deeper understanding of our surroundings. It's important not to struggle with grasping the essence of starting things peacefully and striving for optimal results. If you find yourself dissatisfied with your current self, don't hesitate to bid farewell to the person you once were. Now, you can embark on a rewarding journey aligned with your desires, potentially providing you with abundant fulfillment in this lifetime.

You can find real happiness in life, and it's the main reason to keep going because you have the power to select what you want. You have the opportunity to take a path that allows you to gain a deeper understanding of everything, decide how far you want to expand your ideas, or choose to earn a living from it. Time is also in your control. You can start right where you are and make a living, or you can become an expert, the very best in your field. What you'll come to realize is that we all have innate abilities within us.

Everything in life hinges upon the choices you make and how you direct your energy towards your deepest desires. Alternatively, you have the option to find contentment with your current circumstances. You can follow a simple, less complex path that will grant you a sense of well-being throughout your lifetime. This uncomplicated lifestyle frees you from the complexities of modern living. Instead, you can earn your livelihood in a straightforward manner, liberating yourself from the challenges of the world, and finding clarity and purpose from an early stage in your journey.

Some individuals make the decision to let go of their current circumstances and embark on a new journey. Others find themselves in situations where they have no alternative but to remain stagnant with no clear purpose. It's during these moments that they come to the realization that they must acquire the skills needed to thrive independently. When you set your mind to it, you persistently follow this path until you reach your destination. Perhaps there were other options available, but a sense of profound disorientation led them to believe that facing life's challenges alone was the best course of action. Once deeply committed, your mindset becomes pivotal, and if you maintain disciplined determination, there are no limits to what you can achieve.

You have two choices in life. One is to adapt to what's happening now, while the other is to hold onto your beliefs. You can develop your own way of doing things, different from what everyone else does. In the beginning, people might not listen to you, but over time, your idea will become a central part of your life, expressed through your actions. When your idea clashes with others, stand firm, advocating for what you believe in, without expecting anything but the outcome you desire. Could it be about making a positive impact?

Could you put in effort with affection to witness positive transformations? This is something that truly defines a person. The world isn't progressing in the direction many expect; however, our existence is on a journey towards improvement. The universe longs to witness positive actions. It all began from nothingness, but it was the collective contributions of individuals that continually molded it into something profoundly exquisite. Therefore, endeavor to make a significant impact and labor to reconstruct what has been dismantled. Avoid embracing ideas that fail to bring about any good, as it's greatness that truly matters in the end.

To contribute to positive change and overcome challenges, it's essential to let go of anything that no longer serves a purpose. By doing so, you'll not only establish a business with a clear mission but also create a framework that supports the betterment of the world. What truly matters in the end is your role in guiding the universe towards a brighter future. Therefore, it's crucial to prioritize actions that are vital for life to flourish through your efforts.

Allow the beauty of the world to shine through you. Avoid feeling envious of the wonders of creation and the gift of life. Your character will be expressed eloquently by this, as it's what truly counts when the day concludes. However, many individuals fail to grasp their actions, focusing solely on what they can gain. They forget that the world first wants to see what you can offer before you can receive its rewards.

Always remember to keep this in your thoughts: strive to make sure you have a clear definition of what you're pursuing, and don't be embarrassed that you're considering how the world might benefit from you before you start earning from it. Your actions and your focus should be centered on making a positive impact on life. Ultimately, this is the foundation of your strength, regardless of any external threats. Never forget that if you're willing to do good where it's acknowledged, nothing can permanently obstruct your path.

You may experience a temporary delay in your progress, but it's important to remember that people rely on you to guide them in life. They look to follow your lead, seek a fresh direction, and depend on you to take the wheel, especially when you're enthusiastic about doing meaningful things. Once you grasp the art of accomplishing remarkable feats, everyone will be intrigued by your journey, ultimately making you a pivotal force shaping the future.

You can go as far as the world allows, if you understand how to be a good individual, as you will soon discover. Life will reveal the necessary steps, and with the determination to do what's right, you can continue to harmonize with everything around you. You'll discover the importance of staying attentive, maintaining a keen awareness, and not confining yourself by adopting an approach that aims to exploit others. Always remember that you possess the potential for significance, and to attain a place in the annals of human history is to prioritize people, acknowledging their importance, and offering them something commendable based on your actions.

Your actions for humanity are incredibly important, no matter how small they may seem. When you do things with a kind heart, you can't go wrong. You'll notice that many of life's mysteries will become clearer, and challenges will become less daunting. Sometimes, things may seem tough when you view them from others' perspectives, but when you approach them with your own understanding, you gain clarity. While we aren't naturally inclined to see things this way, it greatly aids in improving your understanding of the world.

You might discover yourself in a situation where you're very certain about nearly everything. However, it's essential to remember that other people's contributions and viewpoints remain significant in shaping our collective identity. It's just that when you view things from your own perspective, your focus tends to be quite narrow. This narrow focus can lead to misunderstandings about life, where some things may not be as crucial for the future we are moving towards, yet they still hold relevance. How can you determine if a particular idea will have a significant impact on society? What is your perspective on this matter?

The primary theme has consistently revolved around the desire to take action, driven by a deep affection for others. Therefore, it's important to ensure that you keep in mind that it's fellow humans you're aiming to bring joy to. Provide them with hope where they may be lacking it. Everyone who approaches you does so with specific needs, and if they don't find what they seek, they might feel quite let down. Nevertheless, if your constant aim is to bring happiness to people, you will never let them down. They will be genuinely delighted with the manner in which you've demonstrated your care for them.

When you're determined to make a positive impact on the world, you'll find that you can never truly lose your way. This is the path where your significance will always be recognized, and where you can discover a sense of fulfillment in your human existence. Sometimes, people lose their sense of purpose as they mistakenly connect running a business with unethical behavior. However, this is not always the case. Successful businesses and innovative ideas often thrive by prioritizing the well-being of communities. When you identify an opportunity to make a positive change, you can be the one to contribute to humanity's healing process. Who better than you to bring about such profound goodness?

If you can see something happening, don't turn your eyes away. Try to demonstrate your concern. Don't wonder why it's happening; instead, think about how you could spend the rest of your life if you seize an opportunity to create something extraordinary. What if such an opportunity never came your way? It doesn't have to be a grand concept; it just needs to be something that answers people's questions and meets their needs, restoring hope to their lives. There's nothing that can't be repaired, no situation that's impossible to overcome. Try to convince people that some good still exists in the world. Alter their perspectives. Just by doing that, you've already done more than enough for everyone to realize that you're here for them.

Chapter Seven

All Alone

When we were kids, we lived in a world that didn't always show a lot of strength and understanding. We saw that when it came to love, women seemed to have more power than men. Women had more freedom in relationships, which was sometimes challenging for men because they found it hard to commit. Whether we liked it or not, we eventually reached a point where we had to stick to our goals. Over time, this started to impact our lives and change how we needed to be together.

If you choose to shoulder your responsibilities and ponder deeply about complex matters, you may eventually reach a point where solitude becomes your companion. Yet, as you approach the conclusion, you might discover that despite your best efforts to rectify this aspect of life, there are no straightforward solutions to set things straight.

Women have their unique perspective on life, which may not always be essential for men when they consider life. They discover strength and bravery in simplicity, whereas men often face challenges in finding purpose and meaning in their endeavors. Until you achieve success, it can be tough to find support from others, leading to an imbalance in our way of life and love, often referred to as "the influence of love on men." This concept has given rise to the notion that during that particular era, it fostered a sense of betrayal among those committed to pursuing certain endeavors aimed at shaping the world.

It's almost like when you tried to start something new, it made the world upset right away, and it felt like you let down your entire life before you even got to where you wanted to go. Not only did you disappoint yourself by changing the way you do things, but it also made everything around you different. What used to be simple is now quite challenging to grasp because of the path you decided to take, and you knew it didn't need to turn out like this.

Perhaps, the reason women hold a special power of love over men could be due to the fact that, at a certain point in our lives, men sometimes struggled with being responsible and honest. It is essential to recognize that without a clear sense of purpose in life, one may not attain the significance they desire, and love may not even come their way. Even if you have a purpose related to creation, it should ideally be straightforward, uncomplicated, and easily understood.

Living a sophisticated lifestyle as a person can sometimes lead to complications in our lives. These complications often arise when we attempt to grasp complex concepts that require intelligence, and in the process, we may find ourselves entangled in matters of the heart. It seems that, as human beings, we naturally gravitate towards simplicity in our relationships. The intricacies of life, rather than complicating everything, seem to touch the very core of our souls and enhance our desire to love one another.

You don't need to live solely for nothing or everything. Instead, strive to live for an adequate purpose. Love appears to play a central role in various aspects of life. Your aim should be to discover a purpose that's comprehensible and attainable by others. Avoid getting stuck at the outset of your journey or staying stuck at a rudimentary level of existence. Don't limit yourself to the extreme edges either. Aim to be at the core of our human experience, an integral part of humanity. This is where true love resides, serving as a predominant theme in our lives and the focal point of all our endeavors.

Isn't it amazing that in the realm of love and relationships, there's a consensus that success is attainable? That you have the potential to embark on endeavors, outperform anyone, and achieve victory. What's even more incredible is the belief that we can accomplish this together while maintaining our deep connection. It's astonishing how we can construct a shared understanding that's both skillful and wholeheartedly cherishes love, allowing us both to always feel embraced within it. This is far better than residing in a place where someone doesn't see the need to link themselves with you because they feel excluded.

Designing a world where a woman can relinquish the authority she once held over matters of love, potentially leading her to betray a man in his quest for companionship, thus preventing the emergence of avoidable situations that erode faith in life and love. This is because if she succeeds in her endeavor, it is ultimately her own soul that she has betrayed.

For a man, there are many things that require understanding, starting from the time when you embark on your career and have to navigate situations where love and integrity might be lacking in the care you receive. This situation can be challenging for both of us. You might possess the strength and clarity of purpose to discern your path and how to reach your goals, but I struggle to perceive what you have seen.

I don't share the same level of faith as you do, and this leads us to see life differently. This difference becomes apparent when we face challenges together. Sometimes, one of us might feel exhausted from our journey, not knowing where the path will take us. However, there are moments when we can carry each other's burdens, making it easier to travel together with a shared vision, strength, and a strong desire to succeed.

One might believe that it should be uncomplicated for a woman to wholeheartedly devote herself to a man, even if she isn't entirely satisfied with every aspect of his life. This is because love, being distinct from the complexities of existence, can transcend such concerns. However, it is crucial to recognize that individuals are shaped by the entirety of their experiences and qualities as they navigate the intricate tapestry of life. Love, being a formidable force, plays a pivotal role in enabling a wide array of possibilities to unfold at the very core of existence.

If someone isn't confident and capable in the core aspects of their life, being there for and loving them through their endeavors can be quite challenging. It may lead to a lot of strain when it comes to maintaining love. This is because the place where people are most sensitive is in the heart of their humanity, and if a woman doesn't see the value in committing herself to something she deems unnecessary, it can make it difficult for her to connect.

In the realm of creativity, we possess the ability to accomplish tasks with the resources available to us. This has consistently revolved around comprehending these different stages, where love has consistently thrived. This revolves around reaching a specific level of dedication in the execution of your tasks. In this context, relationships cannot be imposed but must evolve naturally. The only requirement is for individuals to extend their efforts beyond their prescribed responsibilities in order to effortlessly forge a connection with it.

Instead of feeling neglected and denied the power of love and closure, consider this: when you commit yourself wholeheartedly to your responsibilities and fulfill your duties with dedication, you open the door to discovering a profound love that is shaped by your own comprehension. This genuine affection is uncomplicated, straightforward, and comfortable to embrace and coexist with. It doesn't entail a return to feelings of solitude; instead, it propels you forward, toward the fulfillment of your desires that lie ahead.

When you're striving to build your own comprehension, you might find yourself compelled to explore a new route. It's essential for males to channel their creativity toward positive endeavors, allowing them to contribute to the world's creation. Nevertheless, this endeavor also grants other aspects of life influence, potentially extracting something crucial from every person, regardless of gender. Therefore, it becomes necessary to carefully examine this situation to comprehend how to harmonize the dual aspects of existence: the tangible reality, love, and innovative thought. You must learn how to embrace all your desires while still maintaining commitment and being ordinary in other aspects of our shared existence.

How does it feel to make sense of our own lives and everything we do when we face this kind of reality? Now that we have witnessed the dawn of a new life, the ability to craft something meaningful and articulate the distinctions between then and now comes to light. Back then, we knew little about the world and how to shape our understanding. In the present moment, we exist within our own reality of creation. Despite the possibility of surpassing the ordinary expectations of life, the need for love remains, and all that we have forged or comprehended can influence how we connect with others in the realm of relationships.

In the same world that regular folks live in, you aim to find something meaningful for yourself as you gain recognition. This is where a particular theory comes into play, influencing how we approach commitments and living in harmony. While striving for our personal goals, we may at times grow distant from each other due to the priorities we set, and even the most ordinary world may not provide us with what we seek.

As the kind of people we've chosen to be, we each have our own beliefs and goals in life. There are many ideas in this world about how individuals, both men and women, can be independent and in control of their lives. We desire to have authority over our own destinies, even if it means going without love for a while. What truly matters is making our dreams a reality. We live with a strong determination to shape our own futures. We exist with a burning desire for success, and we don't let others influence our choices.

When we have the ability to control things, we often become focused on ourselves and our desire to lead our own ideas or shape the course of our lives and relationships. Nonetheless, if your ideas don't succeed, it can feel like a personal failure, as genuine love in our lives demands a particular depth of compassion that allows us to integrate into society. To truly become a part of a community through your actions, try not to stray too far from the fundamental principles of life, and aim to be endearing to the people who share the world with you.

To gain acceptance in the lives of others, it's crucial to ensure they have a complete understanding of your actions. This way, they can help mend any potential harm that may result from your decision to distance yourself from fellow humans, as well as from the act of removing individuals from your life in your quest to discover your true essence. However, it's important to note that while this journey will uncover your creative potential, it may not necessarily lead to finding love. Instead, by encouraging others to explore their own paths elsewhere, you create the opportunity for them to discover themselves beyond the confines of your own universe.

Women play important roles in our lives as both wives and friends who deserve a special place in our hearts. If you happen to find yourself involved in a project without a clear goal, they might become quite perplexed about the world you inhabit. It may become challenging for them to connect with you if you delay seeking resolutions for your issues and projects.

As we navigate through life and love, our level of involvement in our own priorities can often lead us to neglect other important aspects, such as love. It's important for us to keep our objectives clear to everyone, and not to conceal our true selves, even when we're deeply engrossed in various activities, as this openness can help others relate to us.

Women often have limited rights, restricting their freedom to do what they want. They often face pressure to please their partners. True love requires them to put aside their own needs and the complexities of the world to discover genuine love hidden in their own lives. However, life's circumstances can give money and other factors control over relationships, weakening commitment to each other. This is especially true during your journey of creation, where productivity plays a crucial role in sustaining your commitment through challenges. If you're not productive enough, you may struggle to withstand these challenges.

If you desire to build a lasting and fulfilling love in your daily life, you may find it necessary to continually invest in both yourself and your relationship, dedicating significant attention to it. Avoid depending solely on your own comfort, as dedicating greater effort and attention can ultimately strengthen your relationships. However, it's worth noting that individuals who have discovered genuine love have, at times, faced allegations of neglecting their partners for personal gratification, which can lead to dishonoring women after an extended period.

We all desire genuine love with a special person. However, life often demands that a person puts in extra effort, regardless of the task at hand, to achieve success and productivity. It's crucial to maintain adaptability in your personal journey, as the realms of love and finances are subject to continuous change, and circumstances can become challenging. This is especially true for those attempting to gain control over various aspects of their lives. Things may not unfold as we initially envision, often diverging from our expectations.

It's important to become skilled at adjusting to different situations, as in a world where a person can't provide for themselves, maintaining love can become challenging. This can have an impact on the individuals you wish to make happy or draw into your life. This applies to anyone seeking a healthy relationship, regardless of their knowledge, background, or identity. It's about the realities of our lives, not just who we are or where we're from.

If you're unable to find the resources to sustain yourself, it can make people feel extremely fatigued and drained during their journey. This might lead to an ongoing search for assistance, with a constant hope that someone comprehends your actions. Eventually, you'll reach a specific point where you realize that you're entirely on your own in this expedition, as you delve deeper into the heart of knowledge.

For a considerable duration, it's crucial not to limit yourself to mere strength in all your endeavors. Even when you find yourself in solitude, it's essential to cultivate a sense of dedication to a higher purpose, something you consider as the ultimate truth. This dedication can significantly influence your life because, undeniably, you cannot fathom the thoughts of others or discern their aspirations based solely on what they comprehend. Therefore, your actions can profoundly shape your identity as you serve this overarching entity, one that is both righteous and sufficient for your entire being.

Living with the hope that there is something or someone you want to accept or understand in your life can sometimes lead you down the wrong path. For your own peace of mind, you might start to believe that there must be someone else who must understand what you're doing. You might keep wishing that you could see the world from that perspective, but it can make your journey more difficult because you might feel overwhelmed. In reality, you are the key to everything you're doing, and you are the reason for everything you're living for.

Having someone else impact your journey isn't just about that specific moment; it has the potential to shape your entire life. Consider the idea that beyond your own experiences, there may be someone capable of providing you with opportunities superior to what you can create for yourself. This situation can be disheartening because when people don't meet your expectations, it can leave you feeling vulnerable and profoundly unhappy. You might question your abilities and whether you can still accomplish what you've set out to do.

When you remove your trust from people and things that exist beyond your immediate surroundings, you gain the ability to comprehend how to attain higher levels of success in the path you've embarked upon. In a perplexing state of mind, you may seek to discover what you define as 'truth' beyond your personal sphere, but if that notion also depends on someone else experiencing it on your behalf, you have yet to fully exercise your freedom of thought, unburdened by any mental constraints.

As you journey down the path of life towards its ultimate destination, you come to understand the significance of various aspects, including those that might have seemed inconsequential before. In this current stage of your life's journey, these elements have emerged as vital foundations for acquiring knowledge about this way of living, as well as for comprehending all that has transpired concerning your overall well-being.

You discovered valuable lessons in life that you might not have known about yourself. Some of these lessons can make you ponder if the path you're on truly influences what you're pursuing, and it's all designed to show you that even when you feel uncertain about certain things, there are moments in your life when you possess the knowledge and precision to handle them.

You should not ignore the fact that you need to face the truth about yourself. Sometimes, you may not appreciate the person you have turned into during your journey. This person might have been fixated on pursuing their desires. Your current circumstances could potentially become a dreadful situation, as you must endure the consequences of your actions and the areas where you have experienced shortcomings thus far.

You may have had a desire to bring about transformations in the world and in your own life. Now, as you embark on your journey, you come to understand that the world is vast, and you've reached a point where you've accomplished quite a bit. However, it seems that your efforts have not yet had a noticeable impact, both on a global scale and in your personal well-being. You find yourself still at the starting point of your path, always remembering that you are a crucial part of this new venture that has begun.

You can't ignore the fact that there were things you didn't like at the start of your life when all these journeys began. What was really important was the truth and depending on the result of your life or the final goal. These are situations that test the truth inside us, and that's where we figure out how to pick our path in this world. But if the truth is the most important thing, then how much do we agree that only what is true about this universe will succeed?

If you answered "yes," it means you've built your foundation on honesty, believing that the truth will ultimately triumph. How much progress have you made in this pursuit, gaining the confidence that your chosen path will lead to success? Have you ever experienced a situation where your commitment to honesty had such a profound impact on your life that it's now deeply ingrained in your core values? Additionally, how many years have you dedicated to practicing and fully comprehending the implications of living an honest life?

Can someone refuse to let you live your life because you've linked your duties to another person? When this connection is intense and powerful, you may find that you don't have to handle everything by yourself. You've placed your trust in someone else, and suddenly, it seems as though a significant burden has been lifted from your shoulders. However, is it essential to be guided solely by what is true or by your own thoughts and creations? Can this approach assist you in bringing to life exactly what you envision in your mind or head?

As you embark on this journey, it might seem like a bit of a time-waster in the grand scheme of being a human. Why? Well, because you're going to have some pretty big dreams and you'll be putting in a ton of effort to make them a reality. But here's the thing: those dreams won't just magically come true overnight. You'll need to give it your all, and along the way, you'll need to get comfortable with the idea of dealing with your current circumstances. It's through your determination and not giving up that your ideas will eventually start to take shape.

The path you've selected will be your sole means of escaping everything, the only route out of this world you truly dislike. As your current situation persists, it raises doubts about whether you're making informed choices or merely gambling. Consider how you view this present world that hasn't offered you anything in life. Despite the fact that you're still here and your entire life may seem insignificant, you remain steadfast in your actions, confident that the moment when your desires turn into reality is approaching.

Everything you've learned so far points toward achieving success. This success is a crucial part of the journey you've embarked upon. It's something you won't be able to endure unless you've figured out how to be successful. Success can be achieved in any situation, whether it's good or bad. It's available for everyone, and even the most complex aspects of life can become much easier to handle when you grasp the keys to success.

However, inside your mind, can you conquer and overcome these negative energies that seek to gain control over your comprehension? Can you reach the part of your new life and vision that you've imagined for yourself? There will always be questions, but one specific question will demand your attention once you've achieved a high level of success: What role do you play in the grand scheme of creation? Are you a part of a universe that possesses vast knowledge and understanding, gained through your own intelligence? You exhibit remarkable thinking abilities, to the extent that you can even devise clever strategies to excel, drawing from your wealth of experience and knowledge of what you're doing.

This is how long the journey can be as you strive to become a better person through your unique way of thinking. It goes on until you fully comprehend everything you're doing. Once you've persuaded yourself about the reality you wish to experience, you need to overcome the mental obstacles that hinder your understanding of what it takes to succeed. It's like a battle inside your mind, questioning if you can truly become the best. So, during the time it takes to reach that point, what actions can you take?

Do you feel prepared for your journey, or do you seek guidance and reassurance from the world beyond, yearning for something or someone to offer comforting words, assuring you that things will eventually turn out well, alleviating your worries? Are you swayed by the world's ongoing realities, or are you the type of person who, in addition to embracing the existence of humanity, has crafted a personal truth that serves as a profound source of motivation for achieving success? Without this inner conviction, it would be challenging to endure the arduous journey toward your ambitious aspirations and ultimately attain your destiny.

Would you ever think about missing out on a chance to witness your initial aspirations? Perhaps due to the challenges you've faced during your creative journey. If you didn't have a clear direction or lacked dedication in pursuing your dreams, you might have prevented yourself from living the life you desired. Nevertheless, you've acquired a wealth of knowledge and skills along the way.

Can you achieve both of your life's initial goals while also maintaining a sense of normalcy or keeping up with everything happening in the environment where you currently live? Is the path you've chosen or started to grasp sufficient to fulfill all your needs in this lifetime and allow you to become the type of person you've recognized within yourself?

Questions may arise and depart, and you have the option to decide whether to stop and hold on to the belief that you've grasped the way this world was in the past. It was indeed a remarkable cosmos, one whose existence you can't refute, albeit not precisely as you hoped or imagined. Have you ever pondered over this query? Is the information I possess adequate for me to attain liberation? It's plausible that creation doesn't require your input because everything was in harmony as it was, and humanity had all the essentials necessary for their advancement in life.

Yes, it has been this way throughout our entire lives. It was sufficient, but perhaps you harbored aspirations for greater creativity and love. You were unwilling to accept a regular, everyday existence. In your relationships, you sought someone extraordinary. However, it's crucial to recognize that all these desires can only manifest once you've finished whatever it is you're currently engaged in. Once you've accomplished that, you can fully savor your newfound understanding and freedom. In either scenario, you will have undergone trials, gained knowledge, and established trustworthiness among many others. Yet, in the end, you will have achieved success on your own.

Does a person's knowledge truly hold enough importance to be the sole foundation for creating value? Is it possible to stand apart from existing norms and return to the real world armed with the vibrant hues of your wisdom, relying solely on that reservoir of knowledge? Even when obstacles attempt to obstruct your path to success, staying loyal to your comprehension and striving to flourish through the lessons you've accumulated thus far. Irrespective of the challenges the present may throw your way, you find the strength to persist with the wisdom you've acquired. Alternatively, you may pause and reflect, recognizing that this may not be the only path to accomplish things, and thus, choosing to look elsewhere and conform to the conventions of humanity.

Our work has a special role in creation. You serve an entity that will depend on you as you go along. Our goal is to achieve this. We want to get to a point where we matter to more than just our own vision and creation. We aim to do it better than many can. We want to reach a level where everything feels effortless. We want to make a difference in different areas of life, even when time is limited for what we want. We're working hard to get to a place where everything about us is in its place. So, in the end, we become a very important part of something bigger than ourselves.

You may sometimes ignore the current moment, even though you're often reminded of how to take control of your life and that it involves dedicating everything you have to your goals. Age should never limit your aspirations; as you grow, you'll witness your dreams coming true and become better prepared for life's challenges. Besides, without this approach, it's challenging to make sense of achieving your desires as you strive for personal growth and self-im-provement.

When things take a turn for the worse, is it easy to openly address the situation with everyone involved? Can you honestly express your feelings even though it might not be a straightforward task to convey your emotions to someone? Without ever attaining success, discussing such matters will never be a straightforward endeavor. This is because your entire life culminates in one crucial aspect: to exhibit the culmination of your actions and the tremendous effort you've invested in achieving it.

You've selected the life you're living from among many options available, and you understood the importance of mastering it thoroughly. When you fully comprehend it, it won't let you down, and you'll live it as you should. Even though you may have faced difficulties at the start, you've now found your footing, enabling you to stand confidently and view the world with the right focus.

What have you given up in your life that meant a lot to you, the one thing that you let go of when things got too hard to comprehend? When you've lost hope in everything you aspired to become, even though you truly desire it, and you can't be the person you once were. Somehow, you're aware that everyone once had a bold dream of becoming someone extraordinary, but can you distinguish yourself from those who once aspired to be greater individuals? Do you possess the determination to approach things in a unique way, can you discover your true self within this expansive universe, and be an individual distinct from the rest of humanity?

It's quite unfortunate how life can change you to the extent where you don't recognize your former self. You carry the weight of this transformation alone because only you truly understand your thoughts. Until you accomplish your aspirations, you won't be able to share with the world what you aimed for in life. There's only so much you can reveal about yourself until you reach a profound understanding, and until then, you live with nothing to cling to. Nevertheless, it brings solace deep within to acknowledge your inherent human potential. Regardless of what you once knew about the world, you've now embraced in your heart the desire to explore a different path that can lead you to success.

When difficult questions arise, and they genuinely desire you to respond thoughtfully, they ponder whether you merely seized opportunities or possessed a clear understanding of your actions, driven by a vision rooted in more than just wealth. Beyond all that exists, opportunities continually emerge for financial gain and a fulfilling life. The question is, can you opt for this simpler path amidst the complex choices that the world offers? Keep in mind that an opportunity has now presented itself.

A single individual has the capability to influence the entire world. They don't need to engage in anything other than pursuing their original purpose. Despite the challenges posed by the passage of time, and the seemingly perpetual difficulties on their journey, where progress may appear elusive, and personal development seems daunting, they may find it challenging to manage these circumstances with great wisdom. It may feel as though the journey of life has been quite demanding on their existing understanding.

As you journey through your small slice of time and space, you may find that the numerous encounters you face often appear overwhelming. It might not be because you're feeling lost or uncertain about whether these experiences will suffice for your entire lifetime; rather, it's the weight of societal expectations and demands that press upon you. When you return to the present moment, you might notice that everyone around you has ventured into their own profound realms, and deep down, it's hard to deny that this somehow saddens you immensely.

Even if you bounce back from a setback, the most crucial question you must answer is whether you will excel in life through all your endeavors. Can you strive to reach a point where you are genuinely content with your accomplishments and the pursuit of your aspirations? Ultimately, you'll need to contemplate whether it's enough to lead an ordinary life or if you aspire to surpass others in your chosen path. How determined are you to pursue this as your ultimate goal or guiding principle? Additionally, keep in mind that success is essential, given that you are a part of this world, where competition is present in virtually every endeavor.

Are you capable of finishing your projects promptly, even when life presents obstacles along the way? Are you willing to dedicate your entire self to make things happen? Your purpose is not to scrutinize the impact of external circumstances on humanity; instead, it's about rectifying them and fostering positivity. There was a time when you were new to this creative journey, unsure whether your endeavors would truly benefit others' well-being.

Even though there's ample evidence pointing towards your future success, you find yourself dwelling in uncertainty. You persistently question whether the goals you've set and the promises you've made will truly have a positive impact on the lives of other people.

You might ponder whether it truly makes a significant impact to have practiced comprehending things and distinguishing yourself from everyone you've ever known. By doing so, you become distinct amidst a multitude, and you challenge your own reality because you are not merely daydreaming about your desires. Instead, you are actively living within the realm shaped by your knowledge. But can you refuse it the chance to shape your own existence and live life on your terms? Is the time almost here, or has it already arrived? Can we start integrating elements of this dream into our daily lives, which is now becoming the architect of our own destinies?

When you're out there, it's just you. You want to show what you understand. You're like an inventor in your own world, and you don't have anyone to help you. You're standing all by yourself. There's only one thing that matters: your ideas. Nothing can replace the way you've been thinking about things.

When you're happy, you'll want to be alone to enjoy it. And when things get tough, you'll be on your own, dealing with it by yourself. If you really know what you're doing, then nothing can ever stop you from achieving success in what you've started. Only when you reach the end will you be safe from all the challenges and negative thoughts that have been bothering you.

Don't just sit around and hope for someone to appear and guide you, acting as if they fully understand your deepest desires. Instead, recognize that the vast cosmos has bestowed upon you the gift of vision, allowing you to perceive your true aspirations. Don't underestimate your worth by saying you lack adequacy when, in reality, you possess everything essential within this grand creation.

Chapter Eight

Power of Love

The distinctions between males and females have created a significant divide that isn't easily bridged. This divide can make some men feel like they lack the ability to easily take charge of their lives, particularly when pursuing their own path of understanding. Is it possible that we have unique duties we must fulfill? Whether you choose to acknowledge them or not, you may find yourself tethered to these responsibilities, leaving you with no alternative but to meet your obligations.

If you don't pay attention to this, many things can become too weak to handle. Would it be fair if everyone had the same duties when it comes to creating things? It appears that only a few people are given these responsibilities, regardless of what you can gain from them. The world of understanding places many demands on someone trying to achieve their ultimate happiness. There is never a moment when something doesn't matter. Everything is important to a fundamental part of who we are and the kind of person we want to become. Sometimes, you might find yourself tied down by your responsibilities, leaving you with nothing but the struggle to overcome difficult situations, almost as if you're under a curse.

You desire to make a meaningful impact and aspire to lead a life filled with greater purpose. Achieving a profound level of understanding is crucial in this pursuit. As human beings, we all experience a variety of challenges on our journeys to diverse destinations, and it's impossible to fully grasp the struggles others are enduring. You are intimately familiar with your own hardships, but you cannot compare them or seek solace in the difficulties faced by others. There is no remedy for this, and it's only just that if you've identified an opportunity to surpass the ordinary, you must rely on your own efforts and abilities.

Have you ever found yourself in a situation where you couldn't move forward, no matter how hard you tried? You kept failing repeatedly. But when you finally reached the end, you realized that any solution would be better than staying stuck. You started to realize that life isn't always easy, and sometimes, it's necessary to take a break and reflect. You began to see that experiences teach us about ourselves and the importance of adapting to who we've become. As you delved deeper into the subject, you matured because sometimes, we embark on paths expecting instant success, but reality often challenges our expectations.

Sometimes, it seems that the journey toward perfection becomes more fulfilling when you have love in your life. Love is when you can count on someone, they support your understanding of life, and they share your vision. Even when facing challenges, having a special person who appreciates your efforts and whom you've invited into your life can make things feel better. You might doubt your worth as you strive to redefine yourself, but as you embrace your true essence, a deeper sense of humanity begins to flourish within you, and this humanity is too precious to be isolated from.

As you acquire knowledge on your journey, someone might discover your usefulness. Even if you sometimes lack confidence in facing challenges, remember that you possess qualities that make you valuable. Don't worry about feeling disconnected from others, as you can never predict what someone might find appealing about you. This realization could occur unexpectedly, long before you reach your destination, leaving you feeling exceptionally valued.

Being all by yourself in this vast world, residing within the confines of your own thoughts, can sometimes make us crave solace and comfort. Yet, when there's neither an external source of support nor a specific person to lift your spirits, upon whom can you depend? This is when we find ourselves becoming our own source of inner fortitude, understanding the expectations the universe has for us, which can serve as our personal route to continuous progress.

You're in a place without any clear shape. You can't go back, and you're becoming a different person now. Trying to look back won't really help you achieve anything either. As you move ahead, you start to see something important: going in either direction doesn't really do anything. Going backward means starting all over again, and that can be pretty tough to understand. There's nothing to grab onto when you look ahead, and the world doesn't make much sense right now. You're just living because you have to, and then you wonder, "What can I do to solve this?"

All of these experiences have not left you with anything other than the ability to love and be loved. Commitments are real, and true love involves holding onto something sincere and deeply connected to our identity. Nobody wants to invest themselves in a relationship that won't lead to a fulfilling life. Consider being a person who has always struggled with finding contentment in their own identity. When everything you do doesn't seem to bring satisfaction, when it feels like you're not appreciated by anyone, and when you're not winning anyone's heart, it can be quite disheartening.

I couldn't ignore my feelings of anger and frustration. It was clear evidence of the life I was currently experiencing, and many things had grown distant from me. There was a time when I loved the world for what it was, but now I couldn't be a part of it, even though I wanted to be. As I reflect on myself, I realize that I'm no longer holding onto anything. Somehow, I understand that the moment has arrived when everything begins to truly matter. Everything around me keeps pushing me, making it hard to find a place where I can settle down, and a lot is happening against my will.

When everything you've been hoping for hasn't happened yet, and you're all by yourself in whatever you're involved in. When you've invested so much in it and there seems to be no way to rekindle your enthusiasm to a certain extent that you're completely clueless. So clueless that if what you're doing were to succeed at this very moment, you'd realize it's not because of your skills, as you had no understanding of what was going on.

Sometimes, our inner desires can lead us to challenging situations. After dedicating a substantial amount of time to a task, you might start feeling tired and consider quitting. Surprisingly, even when you think you've given up, something inside you continues to push forward. Deep down, you've cultivated a strong determination to pursue that specific goal, and this commitment has sparked the formation of a new path.

After investing much effort and making many sacrifices to reach your current position, it's worth pondering whether these sacrifices alone can chart the path ahead. Could it be that we've dedicated so much of ourselves that the route back to our previous state has vanished into obscurity?

Even if you desired to return, there would be nothing left to grasp onto because the past has vanished. Therefore, we continue moving forward. As the path unfolds ahead, where else could you venture when there is nothing behind you? You have lived to witness many things being accomplished and brought into existence through your comprehension. Thus, you wholeheartedly dedicated yourself to observe something coming to life, and since we don't truly lose anything, it has somehow started to take shape in another realm.

When you've journeyed, no matter how tough the world around you seems, and even if you've begun to doubt your chances of achieving success out there. Understanding that you must perform at your best because, despite the efforts we've put in, we can still face consequences for our mistakes. Nothing can be left out; we must consider every aspect, so it's crucial to be cautious in your actions to achieve success.

Love is important. When you don't have love, do you feel like everything is okay? Or do you notice something missing inside you? The issue is that if you always try to find an easy way out of everything, you'll eventually realize that you lack discipline. When you make an effort and do everything that's needed, you'll eventually achieve good results and find success in what you're looking for. Love is not only important right now; it's crucial for the rest of our lives.

There are two paths in life, and neither is guaranteed to last indefinitely. On one hand, there's a path that readies you for any challenge that might come your way, seemingly without end. On the other hand, if we happen to fall short of success, it's essential to remember that we ultimately get what we truly deserve. In such a scenario, you would have earned exactly what you've gained from your efforts.

We often find ourselves feeling like we're being denied the chance to embrace our humanity with ease, especially when we aspire for more from this world and seek to make a significant impact. This feeling becomes particularly poignant when we're faced with demanding and arduous tasks, yet persevere to fulfill and complete them.

When you've witnessed how tough life can be, you might have felt the need to criticize yourself due to the dreams we hold, which sometimes make us overly serious about achieving them. This seriousness can often result in nothing but disappointments eventually. However, if you've followed the necessary steps diligently, can you remain disappointed indefinitely? It's clear that success only demands discipline. Can anyone obstruct your path and tell you that you cannot achieve it? Shouldn't we avoid nothing but shame when we look back on our efforts?

It's important to realize that there's only one way to do something, and that's by doing it exactly as it should be done. You need to be capable of reaching the end, and when that moment arrives, you can proudly declare that you've made every effort within your abilities to bring a particular thing to fruition, even if it wasn't a simple task. The journey towards our destination can be incredibly challenging and may take a long time to complete. So, when you've completed your part, you eagerly await the outcome, which validates all the hard work you've put in.

What should we do when life takes us down an unfamiliar path, and we must decide how to proceed? Perhaps, we should begin by seeking genuine love as our starting point, making it our connection to the world and the lens through which we perceive things. However, what if this pursuit begins to overshadow our creative interests? Moreover, what if adopting such a perspective negatively impacts our comprehension of life? It's possible that we may need to venture forth alone, hoping that solitude will provide us with a clearer understanding of the universe and the right path to take to achieve true contentment in all aspects of existence.

Since we always seek the truth in our lives, especially when it becomes the most important thing to us, we should prioritize honesty. In our quest to create and find our way, it's crucial to discover someone who can support us and guide us out of challenging situations, demonstrating the right path. Sometimes, when we're at our lowest point and have lost our sense of self, this can mark the start of a new life after losing everything we once were.

Perhaps viewing the world through the lens of love might have revealed all that you required to comprehend and witness for a more profound understanding, thereby equipping you for what lies ahead. Although it can be challenging to discover genuine love, when one event leads to another and something crucial is absent, where can you locate it? That sense of gentleness you yearn for before reaching that transformative stage, where your actions mold you based on your pursuit of creation, thus making your authentic aspirations feasible.

You shouldn't allow any obstacles to stop you, no matter what they might be. You need to find a path to move forward. Nowadays, we live in a time when being true to ourselves every day is what helps us attain our deepest desires. I reached a point where I wasn't sure when I'd get there and how much I wanted to reach my goals. I aspired to be the one who discovers and accomplishes everything, including your most heartfelt dreams. What do you think is most important in life?

The star, which brought life into existence where there was once nothingness, holds great significance. All you desire is to have a meaningful presence within the framework of the idea you have conceived. You are the one who occupies a prominent position above all else, no matter how many gates you attempted to unlock. What truly counts is that you eventually found and opened the correct gate, enabling you to progress. And who rewards the effort when you attain success?

Have you been the one accompanying this endeavor since its inception when there was absolutely nothing? Or are you the individual who has illuminated the route out of every predicament, faithfully stationed at the gateway, clutching the keys to existence for all those who arrive fully equipped? For those who sincerely seek a pathway that traverses to the alternate realm of creation, those who have wholeheartedly dedicated themselves to achieving success until the very conclusion. They have meticulously ensured precision in their actions, investing substantial diligence and unwavering confidence in our collective identity. Although we had to make the initial sacrifices, we did so without hubris, paying the requisite toll even before gaining access to that realm.

Something quite peculiar that I've discovered during my journey along this path is the concept of love. No matter how much one comprehends about it, even after unraveling numerous mysteries of creation, love remains elusive. It's as if love exists in a realm distant from our understanding. In moments when one might contemplate quitting or abandoning the path, a lingering fear emerges – the fear of what we might become if we deny ourselves the chance to witness the culmination of our efforts. Therefore, we do not deprive ourselves of the opportunity to gain knowledge and insight, to witness and experience life's outcomes.

We often start without knowing what lies ahead. We step onto a path and continue moving forward, sometimes neglecting those who depend on us. Sometimes, you must understand that to take care of yourself, you may need to release certain external burdens. You desire to support everyone who relies on you and whom you love, but you also have a responsibility to nurture your own growth. Our past experiences shape us, and we cannot ignore them. We must live with them while striving to be there for those who depend on us the most and whom we care for deeply.

You feel a deep understanding and a strong desire to support not only your family but also all of humanity because they hold significant importance in your heart. Since we can't all know everything about life, those who possess knowledge should help those who haven't been as fortunate in grasping the meaning of things. These individuals are among the ones we aim to care for wholeheartedly, giving our all to their well-being and growth.

At one time, there was just me, and there were others on the opposite side. Those others meant more to me than anything else in the world. Without them, life would feel utterly shapeless and void. They bring a sense of completeness to the world we aspire to build. Remember, you're not entirely alone. You might be temporarily blocking out everything else to concentrate on what requires your immediate attention. However, everyone will hold significance in the emerging order.

Even when faced with challenging circumstances, it's important to understand the probabilities we must overcome. These odds are present in every aspect of our lives. Sometimes, we hinder our own progress and prevent our goals from materializing. We should avoid underestimating the idea of love. Love is not limited to newcomers in our lives; it also encompasses those who have always been by our side, those who have been with us for a long time. There's no need to overlook these individuals.

Sometimes, you might lose touch with the reality we all live in and the many people you care about. But eventually, you must find your way back to them because they are important. Not everyone is meant to possess this kind of knowledge. A strong desire for understanding can disconnect you from the life that is happening now, making you feel empty and vulnerable to everything around you. Gradually, I came to realize that I wasn't just exploring the world for myself; I was carrying everyone with me. Together, we ventured to discover new things beyond the gate. I wasn't walking alone; I had them within me.

If I had love, it played a significant role in my life. Many people depended on me to teach them how to find happiness through love because I had guided them this far. I've come a long way to reach the heart of creation, and I've always remembered the importance of treating others with honesty. I've learned not to underestimate the value of people in achieving your life's desires. Your actions have far-reaching consequences, and if you disregard them, it can impact others. Now, you probably understand how many people rely on your genuine love and care out there—innocent lives depend on your sincerity, and it matters to each and every one of them.

Can we repair the things that have been damaged, or can we only mend the things that are broken? We gain a lot of knowledge by following the path of creation, and we are motivated to become better individuals because we are not the first or the last in this journey. If someone is doing what feels right for them, what would you do in response? How would you commit your life to all the opportunities that exist out there? It's difficult to predict exactly who you would become, especially if you prioritize what truly matters to you rather than what is deemed important by society. So much of life is centered around pleasing people and addressing their needs.

What matters to all people is what leads to the same destination you desire, but you may prefer to pursue it in your unique way. What do you possess that differs from what everyone else has? After deviating from the usual path, when you return to life, you'll find that much has transformed, and things are not as they once were.

While we all must adhere to the passage of time, it is imperative to recognize that dependence on inconsequential matters should be avoided. To make a meaningful impact on humanity, one should wholeheartedly commit themselves to endeavors that hold significance. Concentrate your efforts on the essential aspects of existence. By doing so, your accomplishments can transcend conventional limits, ultimately bringing substantial benefits, possibly even surpassing the anticipated boundaries of reality.

Every creative endeavor offers something unique that shows you've devoted yourself to a meaningful purpose. When you embrace the results as your greatest achievements, they can shine like a bright star in your life. How can you explain the time you've spent away from what truly matters, even though it meant so much to you, and you weren't able to be a part of it?

It's even more challenging when you were aware of the actions you needed to take, but you had to figure out a way to find contentment in observing events from afar, patiently awaiting their fulfillment. It's truly disheartening if you can't attain your life's desires, especially when you had to make significant sacrifices that prevented you from aligning with a particular group that held different beliefs from your own, since you held steadfast to your unique ideas. You persist in your efforts, firmly believing that a substantial reward lies deep within, waiting to manifest, and that's what holds the utmost importance for the rest of your life.

You may have forgotten how to enjoy life and may have considered settling for something beneath your worth, especially after putting in so much effort. The journey towards self-discovery and recognizing your own value has been a lengthy one. When you finally reach the destination of self-awareness, you realize that you are deserving of everything that resides within you. You cannot deny yourself what you have earned through your hard-fought struggles.

The thing to understand is that we can't predict what will happen in the future, and we can't be sure if we'll achieve the goals we want to achieve. When you desire something but don't know how to get it, you need to focus on creating value to attain it. Deep down, you may feel frustrated because you have to work really hard to find solutions even when it seems impossible. You have to uncover the truth in challenging situations, even though it can be tough. However, you shouldn't give up on yourself. You know this is crucial to achieving your goals, and that's why you must persevere.

We each have our unique ways of creating things, and your approach has distinct characteristics. These differences reflect in many aspects of our work. However, we should ponder: can we motivate ourselves to achieve our goals even when we're not fully prepared? Is it possible that the right time to act is always now, and we sometimes choose the easiest path? At times, we resist letting go of our past selves, but if you don't pursue endeavors aligned with your ambitions or establish clear objectives for achieving success, it becomes challenging to evolve.

When you are in a clear and focused state of mind, you can discern when something has been done exceptionally well and when it falls short. You have the ability to perceive and acknowledge when additional effort is required to achieve perfection in your work. The key here is your precise understanding of the situation, allowing you to sense the need for increased dedication. Your extensive knowledge about creation and your message for the world suggests that by investing more time and wholehearted commitment, you can express yourself more effectively.

Sometimes, when your work doesn't fully inspire you, you should ponder:

Where is the artist within you during this process? It's evident that something is amiss. Imagine it as striving to become the best version of yourself. If you visualize yourself as the ultimate role model and put in concentrated effort and time, you can watch your self-image take shape. Even though there are moments when you may feel lost, remember that you are the one molding your own existence. To succeed, channel your energy both spiritually and physically. When you've pinpointed your focus, continuously refine and enhance your identity through your creative pursuits.

At the conclusion, make sure to express gratitude towards those individuals who have consistently supported you throughout your journey. Show appreciation for the abundant affection they've bestowed upon you. Demonstrate your caring nature and the deep significance they hold in your life. Remember, you're not enduring this artistic existence for the sake of others; you're thriving within it. Therefore, embrace a heart filled with kindness. As we embark on this journey, let us bring our full selves, infused with creativity and intelligence, and fortified by sound reasoning. For many of us, this endeavor has always revolved around a fundamental idea: the creation of our lives and the utilization of our talents.

There are various methods for accomplishing tasks, but the one that holds the greatest significance is the one you've crafted for yourself. If you wholeheartedly dedicate yourself to it, employing all the skills you've acquired thus far, you have the potential to achieve remarkable feats, for it is the sole path devoid of bounds. Always remember to exhibit unwavering determination throughout your involvement with it, as it holds greater importance than everything else in existence. If you can ensure that you're pursuing what genuinely interests you, all you need to do is emanate that passion for it, as people are most drawn to love above all else.

Discovering a profound passion within yourself means embracing the vast reservoir of love that surrounds us all. This relentless devotion to life's journey is a treasure beyond measure. Cultivate a realm overflowing with benevolence, from which every soul can glean valuable insights. Share your wisdom with the world, and watch as it gravitates towards this radiant beacon. Your identity matters less than the ideals you embody, so continue to shower the world with the radiant aura of genuine love and unwavering dedication. Humanity is drawn to the enigmatic, the uncharted, and the transformative. People yearn for fresh perspectives that enlighten their own understanding of self.

Throughout your entire lifetime, it's crucial not to hold back on your creativity. Understand that as you invest time and effort in nurturing your innovative ideas, there will eventually come a moment to present them to the world. This is the fundamental essence of motivation - the journey of self-development, ensuring that you're the best version of yourself for all to admire. For the majority of your existence, this is what you'll be acknowledged and celebrated for. Though uncertainty may linger along the way, rest assured that as you near complete mastery of your craft, you'll witness people attempting to connect with your work, even though it may drain their energy. This is merely a testament to the final trials that pave the way for everyone to reap the rewards of your success.

This is the stage where we often dedicate the majority of our lives. It's the development stage, where we come up with ideas that will become part of what we create. We carefully select the ones that fit into this creation and leave behind the ones that don't quite match. Only the ideas that truly reflect the reality of our world get a chance to be unveiled to the world, shining brightly for everyone to see their triumphant journey.

Can you picture the act of choosing what truly matters in this world, something that will genuinely become a significant part of your life without causing harm? The creative aspect of your work defines your identity; you've discerned what the world craves, and you've succeeded. Nothing holds greater importance than this, and no one can ever snatch away your profound understanding. We may have entered this life by various routes, but once you've achieved it, the outcome remains consistent.

Don't worry about being different. Many people who found important things started just like you. There may be some variations here and there, but the key to success is the same for everyone. So, step out and demonstrate what you've become. Even though you might face challenges, you can find ways to protect yourself based on your achievements. When you complete your work with exceptional creativity, it enriches life for everyone. Those who reject this idea will also be excluded from the creative process.

You can never predict the exact factors that might propel you toward your destiny. Alternatively, you might independently attain the highest level of achievement through your own comprehension. However, there are moments when we take varying approaches to life. It is possible that you may not always be the best, and that's perfectly fine. You do not need to emerge victorious in every situation consistently. With your existing knowledge, you can navigate your path out of any circumstance until you ultimately achieve success. You can focus your concerns on the necessary actions required to shape your life as it should be.

You have indeed achieved this. Your hard work is evident, and you are now at your destination. So, don't give up; continue your efforts until you reach the ultimate level of determination. Keep addressing matters until you have fully fulfilled your purpose.

A person's dedication and capacity to grasp things can open doors to many opportunities and help you learn more about yourself. Therefore, strive to carry out tasks with precision, demonstrating your commitment. Additionally, cherish and keep close those you hold dear, show them deep affection, and prioritize self-care, even occasionally putting yourself first.

Chapter Nine

Never Too Young

When it comes to relationships in this particular lifestyle, many things become challenging to grasp. You start to become intertwined with all your actions, and love, which is a crucial aspect of human existence, demands a distinct approach. The knowledge you once had about the world undergoes a transformation, and if you fail to comprehend how reality functions, you may not reach your ultimate goal.

Many things in life are shaped by the knowledge you possess. To discover a suitable partner and experience happiness in a romantic relationship, you may need a specific degree of comprehension. The difficulties you encounter on the journey to establishing connections can significantly impact your overall quality of life. Your approach to managing your personal matters can have a profound effect on your well-being going forward. Achieving contentment with your true self may necessitate a committed and focused approach. More-over, everything you employ for enjoyment can undergo a transformation in its significance, and it's rare for someone to perceive you exactly as you desire to be loved.

When you lead a life that involves interacting with others, you become an alternative choice, and your actions may not align with your lifestyle and love perspective. In this new approach to life, it's crucial to remain vigilant because people may have opinions about whether you fit into their lives or become a part of who they are. If life ever provides a solution to what you're pursuing, although it may not be an effortless path to your goals, you can certainly agree with that. However, it will now become a way through which you can find respite from the complexities of this world. It's worth noting that this type of engagement requires dedication and a thorough understanding.

To guide yourself toward a positive path, you must possess the ability to clearly envision the impact and significance that your actions will have on both your life and the lives of others. Even though you may exert significant effort in maintaining contentment, achieving this requires a steadfast commitment, especially in a world that can often seem perplexing and challenging to comprehend.

Many factors play a role in determining the results of our hard work. These factors not only reflect our dedication but also serve as a gauge for the success of our endeavors. Relationships and money serve as the ultimate rewards for all that we strive to accomplish. Failing to attain these two objectives may indicate that our current pursuits lack purpose, making it challenging to find meaning in our endeavors. It's important to acknowledge that you cannot manage everything in the world simultaneously while handling all your personal matters. Nonetheless, it is essential to establish a recurring set of actions that can yield positive outcomes with the resources at your disposal.

To harness the power of creativity effectively and gain control over life's circumstances, it's important to apply your understanding and knowledge to create meaningful outcomes. Avoid getting trapped solely in the requirements of the creative process. Instead, consider initiating projects using your wealth of insights. Don't let situations persistently push you into a corner where you have nothing tangible to demonstrate.

In the realm of deeply thoughtful individuals, there arises a profound comprehension—an understanding that springs forth from the intricate tapestry of connections and bonds we share with all living beings. Yet, when looked at through the lens of creativity, life serves as a canvas for the myriad perspectives, viewpoints, and notions held by the diverse multitude inhabiting this world. It's conceivable to ponder whether there exists an element beyond what one presently comprehends, but it is we who craft the entirety of our existence. Whatever you designate as your primary pursuit invariably yields the fruits of your diligent endeavors.

Many individuals embarking on a creative journey often find themselves constrained, unable to fully embrace normality in various aspects of their existence. They frequently undergo assessments that scrutinize their comprehension at every conceivable level. Should one fail to exhibit traits such as faith and courage, they may transform into something unrecognizable compared to their original self since time immemorial.

Yes, it's possible to be influenced by many ideas crafted by others, but if you're truthful with yourself, life can guide you toward uncovering your genuine purpose based on the things you've found fascinating. Resist the numerous forces that aim to consume your knowledge, even though there are many things in the world that pose a danger to a unique mind and attempt to deprive you of everything. This happens only because when you truly understand what you're pursuing, you transform into a magnetic force that draws you back towards enlightenment.

The world offers everyone equal chances to achieve their dreams. However, it's only when a person becomes extremely dedicated and steadfast in pursuing their goals that they can turn those opportunities into reality. So, if, unfortunately, you have chosen a path that others have already trodden, it might be a bit challenging to distinguish yourself from the crowd. You may feel the pressure of competition. But as you persist on this well-trodden path, eventually, you'll reach a point where your unique skills and expertise shine, granting you a chance to reap the rewards of your efforts.

Working in a difficult situation can be quite tough because both sides have their own ideas that aim to challenge each other. This might turn into a competition, but it's disheartening when one side intentionally tries to harm the other. Now, the goal is to prevent each other from reaching their objectives. This can be a significant setback, especially if you're new to this level of existence. You might even consider altering the goals of your idea or creation.

In the realm of relationships, it's crucial to approach your actions with thorough consideration. Failing to do so may put at risk something essential for achieving true happiness. When you make compromises that harm fellow humans, your relationships can undermine the entirety of your life, leaving you perpetually unsatisfied in your quest for genuine love that fills your heart with contentment.

Happiness can be found in following your path, even when time tries to hinder your progress. Don't let it affect you on a personal level. Instead, focus on maintaining the intentions you set from the start. Don't let your heart falter, and don't get lost in ideas crafted by others. This is a common challenge, dealing with powerful concepts created by determined inventors who pushed through to realize their visions.

They let their ideas develop to a specific point where they solidified them, by not opting for an easy path toward their goals. This is a common occurrence—you abandon your original creation and yield to inventions crafted by individuals with clear visions who resist being swayed by anything that comes their way. You then become susceptible to someone else's concept, and before you realize it, you find yourself engulfed, witnessing your world transform into something unintended from the outset.

When you make money your main goal, you shift your focus and start pursuing financial success. This can lead to your values being swayed by money. Sometimes, it might seem unimportant, but in the end, it becomes significant. However, it's not guaranteed that everything you achieve aligns with your original intentions.

Sometimes, when you start on a path, you might get led in a different direction than what you initially planned. However, if you hold onto the idea that inspired you in the first place, you might discover that your life is molded by the way you've crafted your own world. As time passes, you can position yourself profoundly without anyone comprehending the journey that got you there, only to realize that your achievements came from diligently pursuing your goals with patience.

It's never too soon to strive for success in even the most intricate of concepts. You can achieve victory in any endeavor you undertake, right from your current position. You're not youthful forever, so don't settle when things aren't going well. Keep your mind active, constantly questioning what you're doing and why you're doing it, considering what you aim to gain. Meanwhile, ensure you're not letting life slip away without purpose.

As you find yourself in your current situation, you might be pondering why it's important to stick to your plans and how you can reach your ultimate success. Nevertheless, it's crucial to recognize that you shouldn't allow anything to alter your goals. Instead, strive to develop a clear vision that will enable you to draw the finest outcomes in whatever endeavor you are pursuing.

Why do we need to nurture certain ideas? Sometimes, you can't just stumble upon something and instantly make it amazing, or simply integrate it into people's lives. It's important not to believe that the world lacks intelligence to naturally progress on its own; everyone has their own goals and aspirations, and they're all striving to achieve something in their lives. To gain recognition for your ideas, you must rise above the ordinary existence that everyone shares and reach a particular level that few can attain. This is when you've truly created something noteworthy. Attempting to pressure others into understanding your ideas can transform a good concept into a destructive force that aims to engulf people.

Knowing what you must do requires discipline. It means acquiring the skill to nurture your ideas without straying into the wrong path due to money's influence. If you can successfully handle this, you'll evolve into a prosperous inventor. Nevertheless, there might come a point when the world appears to have little more to bestow. Nonetheless, occasionally, as individuals, we owe it to ourselves to execute tasks meticulously. Love can't be genuine if you haven't remained faithful to life's essence.

Indeed, we all desire a straightforward solution, hoping to effortlessly reach a destination where we are completely free from the complexities of our world. Nevertheless, it's crucial to recognize that there isn't a straightforward route that can safeguard us against a multitude of potential mishaps if we yield to something that doesn't align with our true selves. Releasing prematurely the one thing that is destined to become your guardian could potentially turn out to be one of the most significant errors you've ever made. Instead of merely reaping the benefits without comprehending the underlying principles, endeavor to gain a profound understanding of how circumstances manifest in your life. Avoid merely accepting whatever comes your way, as such choices could lead you to inadvertently act against your own intentions.

Sometimes, we must take a moment to ponder and scrutinize the decisions we make. Why engage in actions that we're fully aware will lead to unfavorable consequences or adversely impact our goals? Choices bear repercussions, so why opt for courses of action we know are morally unsound? It's vital to wholeheartedly dedicate ourselves and establish a firm commitment to follow a specific path, ensuring we comprehend that straying from it could jeopardize our ultimate objectives.

You can lead a comfortable life when you're aware that you don't need to engage in activities that might negatively impact or alter the results of your original intentions. There's this particular task that, if pursued, goes beyond your responsibilities and, in doing so, alters the essence of all the goals you've dedicated your entire life to accomplishing.

These paths can provide a relatively straightforward solution to a complicated problem, but they may not always prove entirely reliable over time. Your commitment to a particular discipline is key to attaining success. How much importance do you place on your life? It's all about cherishing your ideas so deeply that you never want to get caught up in such setbacks.

In life, you might encounter circumstances that challenge your beliefs. Sometimes, you might face difficulties and setbacks, but it's essential to be ready to lead your life with your core values close to your heart. By appreciating your own insights and goals, some of which may merely be inquiries, you can question the nature of your existence as an individual. Does the timing and manner of your success truly matter, or is the most important thing achieving happiness and personal freedom? What aspects of this world will you find joy in, considering that nothing is exclusively reserved for you?

Is success connected to surpassing others, or does it relate to the type of work we engage in, enabling us to excel compared to others? It's important to ponder such inquiries, recognizing that life rarely provides solely for one person. Individuals attain accomplishments in various ways, and to them, these achievements represent success. What truly counts is that they have achieved their goals, and it has granted them the lifestyle they aspired to.

You will observe and understand what actions to take. As a young individual, certain opportunities may have eluded you. Nevertheless, when you gaze beyond, you aspired to attain similar objectives. You sought a life that would become a source of pride, owing to the wisdom you would employ in its pursuit, which would serve as a testament to your character. It remains a reality that at your core, you are just like any other human being, driven by the same desires, albeit distinguished by your exceptional comprehension, leading to remarkable achievements.

You didn't always have the opportunity to dedicate your life to a single purpose. However, the moments you missed out on have played a crucial role in shaping the kind of person you aspired to be. It's just that there are aspects of life where you're just like everyone else, and some opportunities might have slipped by because you never had the chance to pursue them, even though you should have been involved.

Is it too difficult to give up some things in order to have what you truly love? You know that you want a lot from life, but it feels like you're experiencing many challenges. Somehow, you act as if you're on a noble mission, trying to influence people to follow your way of doing things, introduce new trends in their lives, and change their behavior. However, deep down, you're going through a lot. Have you ever questioned the authority you've granted yourself as a young person? Why have you assumed so much power? Is it genuinely reflective of who you are, or did you simply choose to take advantage of and exploit other people?

Perhaps you've recently discovered a specific need in people's lives and made a decision to address that need. But what motivates you to take this path? Is it driven by compassion or financial gain? If your primary goal is to amass wealth, many others share that ambition as well. What sets you apart and makes you believe you deserve an opportunity to lead a distinct way of life? Pursuing a goal without a foundation of genuine care for humanity might eventually reveal a stark contrast between your perception of the world and reality. In the competitive landscape you might encounter, especially if your focus isn't on people, a sincere commitment to creating a positive impact will always stand strong against competing objectives.

To nurture a thought or craft a profound notion, delve into the realm where you aspire to enact positive change in the lives of others. It's crucial to recognize that the resilience of humanity surpasses common perceptions of fragility. Deep within, individuals possess remarkable strength, capable of shielding themselves when confronted with uncomfortable truths. When endeavoring to shape enduring contributions to our world, even if your intentions have not been rooted in benevolence and affection, people can readily discern your underlying motives.

You are aware that some people may experience exploitation and face negative consequences due to your success, which may result in their needs being compromised. If you constantly take from them without giving back, they will eventually learn to protect themselves. Therefore, even before you launch your idea, consider the importance of who these individuals truly are. Humans possess a natural intuition that allows them to anticipate events, and they have an innate shield that guards them against negative energies and influences. Their existence holds significant meaning in certain aspects of reality.

If you're all about solving their problems, you'll notice them welcoming you and progressing alongside you. So, as soon as you introduce your idea to the world, your rewards stem from guiding them to become better individuals. You won't be living by imposing your ideas on others anymore. Instead, your life will revolve around aiding them with your own innovations. Now, picture a scenario where you're not focused on healing; you start building a world that only benefits you by revealing others' shortcomings. However, if caring is what fills your heart, your financial success starts measuring how many lives you positively influence.

When you get ready for the world, it's important to ensure that you're preparing yourself to make a positive impact. It doesn't matter how old you are; you're never too young for various situations where you'll be required to take on specific roles or tasks. The duties you assume should demonstrate your readiness to make a meaningful contribution to the global community.

However, as you journey through life, you might find that you're not as young as you once were when you embark on the path to becoming more human. This path may lead you to a life where it feels like you're falling behind in many aspects, and it can be challenging to bridge the gap once again. You might discover that you've lagged behind in various areas, and you'll yearn to engage in activities that help you catch up. This route is quite unusual, and while others are occupied with their own lives, you'll be busy pursuing something distinct that may not be considered progressive for a while.

To succeed, you must use your creativity and unique perspective, as you won't simply follow the crowd. Discovering your purpose may come easily, but the real challenge lies in putting in the effort and transforming your ideas into productive creations. You will encounter obstacles that will help you learn how to make your entire life meaningful to you. This may require you to boost your determination and work hard to achieve everything you desire.

No matter why you're here, whether it's to help people get better or not, you must be ready to make them understand your point of view. Some individuals have been gone for a long time, and they don't want any changes; they prefer things to stay as they are. So, whatever your idea is, don't alter its goals and outcomes, even if you've faced a few rejections. Stay reliable and carry out precisely what needs to be accomplished. Even if it's an idea that appears highly significant and more essential than anything else, don't modify its final result, as people might appear to be very eager.

You're following a certain path that could turn out to be the most precious gift you've ever received, and you don't want to regret who you'll become in the end. It's not just about valuing your work; it's also about cherishing your life, understanding that deep within, you hold a love for yourself that goes beyond what it takes to achieve. You deeply value the ideas that have helped you discover your true self, and these ideas have played a significant role in shaping the person you are today—a person who lives by strong morals and genuine values. You once wished for the world to forgive you for not being perfect, but now you strive for perfection through your understanding and discipline, and by doing so, you've touched the lives of many.

Living such a life often becomes challenging due to the necessity of gaining knowledge primarily through personal experiences. Consequently, instances may arise when we find ourselves compelled to participate in activities we consciously understand should be avoided. During these moments, we can become perplexed about the path we should follow, ultimately succumbing to ideas that hold little significance. When does the realization dawn on you regarding the importance of adhering to the commitments you've made to yourself, even if they do not align with your true identity?

Appreciating the inner you that resides deep within is essential. It's crucial to recognize that as you mature, you should refrain from making the same mistakes repeatedly. There comes a moment when you must make firm decisions about everything you engage in and the outcomes they bring. Even as the world continues to evolve in its own way, it's important to ensure that your life is just the way you want it to be.

Time may leave you feeling disappointed, but don't let those disappointments guide you towards making poor decisions. Sometimes, fear can sneak into your thoughts when things don't seem to be going your way. Maybe you're unsure about the path you've chosen in life and how success will come your way. However, don't let the world's pressures trouble you, as you can choose to be different from those who take from others. From the beginning, decide not to let anything push you into unnecessary actions, and let that decision be one of the choices you've made wisely about who you are.

Don't let situations you didn't create control you. Be absolutely sure that you're now in a position where you can make all your decisions confidently. Make sure you have no regrets about who you've been in the past, who you are now, or who you'll be in the future. Embrace what you have because it's exactly what you wanted, and you wouldn't change it for any reason. We learn a lot as we go through life, but there are some things you'd never do. Instead, you might choose to remain in challenging situations without a clear way out, pretending to be lost in any circumstance.

Keep in mind that your life is always shaped by the person you've been since the very start, a result of the choices you've made. You don't want these choices to become obstacles. It's essential to be confident in staying true to yourself and not making excuses for your past. Hold onto your inner self and don't dwell on past occurrences. Why let yourself stray from the path you've chosen?

How can you continue living with yourself if you ever engage in actions that might put your entire life at risk? It's important to sincerely pray with all your heart that even if what you thought was right turns out to be partly wrong, you can still discover a new purpose. However, the path you have chosen often becomes a significant part of your identity. This is one of the many aspects that shape us as individuals. Your true self, seeking growth and fulfillment, should remain unshaken by doubt. Ensure that your decisions result from your diligent efforts. Whether your experiences have molded you into the person you are today or if your activities have played a significant role, remember that the person you have become is a reflection of your authentic self.

Having that ability can bring you a sense of calm, even in the face of potential failure in your endeavors. It means you'll always have a guiding light that aims to bring out the positive aspects in everything around you. Armed with this knowledge, even when dealing with intricate challenges, which are a natural part of life, you can continue to draw positivity from the world around you.

Don't allow yourself to be held back. Face situations head-on and grant yourself the freedom to live your life, whether you're certain or unsure about being correct. Embrace the inner self that emerges from the choices you make, and you'll find yourself blessed. Develop the ability to turn your gaze away from the difficulties you encounter, and maintain a sense of calm. Remember, you hold value in the person you've become, even if you've experienced disappointment from those you admire.

You might feel very scared for your life if you've changed a lot and don't know where you fit in now. There are things you'd rather not know or go through because you want to be the way you are, and there are things you want no part of. But when it's all said and done, you should see yourself as someone really important, and you shouldn't let anything or anyone change you or make your life worse, no matter what challenges the world throws at you.

Choosing to listen to your heart might sometimes make you feel as if you've lost sight of your own significance in the grand scheme of your life. Nevertheless, remember that you are the most important person to yourself, and your own well-being should always hold greater importance than anything else. Regardless of how challenging your circumstances may seem, never abandon the essence of your humanity, and be mindful that neglecting your responsibilities due to a lack of integrity in your choices will eventually catch up with you.

You may discover motivation and return to your everyday life, where you encounter the usual stress that's been a constant presence. However, it's crucial to remember that your significance lies within yourself, especially when you may perceive your existence as lacking meaning as you observe the external world. This feeling is a construct of your own making; you aimed to endure it, but it shouldn't harm you or the valuable inner self that you've always possessed, a self that holds immeasurable worth.

You had an expectation that the coming day would bring clarity, but when you awoke the following morning, you found yourself confronting the same harsh truths you encountered the day before. It's essential to understand that nothing will vanish instantly; rather, it will persist for an extended period. As you continue on this journey, each day will contribute to your spiritual and physical development, and at some point, you may experience a sense of loss deep within yourself.

Perhaps you may have experienced setbacks for the moment, but it doesn't mean it's the end of the road for you. You still have the opportunity to rebuild your inner self. The journey ahead may be longer than you initially thought, and various events will occur along the way. However, during this process, you will also evolve, just like every other human being does. Even if challenging circumstances make you feel trapped, don't allow disappointments to hold you back. When the time comes to move forward, you will need to progress alongside others and seize your share of life from the opportunities that arise.

It's unfortunate that you wished for everything to occur rapidly, and you're feeling the stress of time ticking away, with occasional reminders that you might miss deadlines. What you truly need is to ensure that you don't solely concentrate on achieving your goals; instead, you must also strive to evolve into the person you've aspired to be. Although it may seem at times that your efforts lack purpose, it's essential to maintain some belief in yourself.

Always keep in mind that you have a purpose, and you know you've embarked on an incredible journey, even if you've taken action in the past or perhaps you haven't taken any steps yet. This endeavor could ultimately demonstrate your value and your potential to excel. Convince yourself that you fully understand what you're committing to, and you've undertaken this path because you possess the skills and abilities to attain greatness.

Chapter Ten

Man in Arts

Many individuals possess captivating life narratives and a deep under-standing of their identity. However, there are instances when they struggle to convey these stories in a universally appealing manner, and this isn't always something that can be rectified easily. There exists only a singular opportunity to seize the spotlight and be heard by a global audience, and the root issue might be a lack of self-assurance. We often fail to establish a meaningful connection with our inner selves and to concentrate on the facets that require exploration within our own beings. When we neglect self-examination, we overlook a crucial component of our creative endeavors, which happens to be the most profound aspect capable of eliciting the finest qualities within us.

The most important thing you should pay attention to is finding a unique perspective that helps others understand who you are. You are not lacking in value. Each of us possesses something significant to share with everyone. People could benefit from listening to your life experiences, using them as motivation and a valuable source of inspiration. If you ignore yourself and focus on sharing things unrelated to your true self, you miss the mark. Your own life should be the center of attention.

Each person's unique experiences have the potential to become fascinating stories. You possess incredible significance that may surpass your wildest imagination. The emphasis on others' lives is just one aspect of feeling lost. It's possible to unintentionally imitate something deeply personal in someone else's life, which might not have much relevance to the broader world when seen through your perspective.

So, how can we craft a memorable narrative? First and foremost, don't underestimate the fact that you are at the center of attention, and your presence holds more significance than everything else out there. Sometimes, we get so caught up in emulating someone else's life that we overlook the most valuable aspect of creativity. In reality, all you need to do is search for the core essence of your true self and focus on nurturing it.

No matter what it might be, it could be something that sparks your creativity and motivation. It doesn't have to be a cheerful aspect of yourself to make a great story. It can be something you feel should be shared. There are numerous life experiences we can exchange with each other. We can gain valuable insights from them, and they can serve as a source of motivation and inspiration. Moreover, many people might be able to relate to these experiences. By centering your narrative on your identity, it can become something that holds significant meaning, especially for those who have found an opportunity to showcase their talents on a global scale.

We often stumble due to our own weaknesses. Sometimes, we find ourselves lacking the motivation to explore our unique tales and distinct perspectives. Instead, we become captivated by the lives of others, ultimately adopting their lifestyles as part of our own creative journey. This can result in the act of copying someone else's work, hindering our ability to reach our full potential. While it's perfectly fine to draw inspiration from others, it's crucial not to fixate solely on them. After all, the one person you truly understand is yourself. When it comes to the realm of art, approaching it from this perspective can yield profound insights into creativity. By focusing on yourself, you can become the best version of yourself in your creative endeavors. Inspiration will never run dry when your own unique perspective is your primary muse.

Whenever you touch something, you have the power to inspire countless people. Deep within you, there lies a wellspring of wisdom, and you possess a vast reservoir of knowledge. All you need to do is recognize these qualities within yourself. It's possible to doubt your abilities and place your faith in others, but the real source of inspiration lies within you. By delving into the depths of your soul, you can uncover incredible talents that will reveal a lot about who you are. The inspiration you seek resides within you; you are not the conclusion of your journey but the inception of a new chapter. As we journey through life, we start as students, gaining experience and gradually understanding how to harness our artistic talents more effectively.

Understanding someone's true intentions for their life is a mystery, so the key to expressing yourself freely is through your own life experiences. You have the opportunity to be authentic, even if your journey has been filled with challenges and disappointments. It's important to remember that you don't have to be unhappy all the time. What truly counts is your ability to discover a unique perspective that can make others appreciate and embrace who you are. Being an artist offers the wonderful opportunity to take these narratives and present them in a compelling manner that resonates with people worldwide, fostering love and comprehension.

You can possess all the essential elements you require and still not manage to leave a lasting impression on others. This can happen if you haven't discovered your true talent and haven't figured out how to effectively share it with everyone around you. To become a proficient artist, it's crucial to unearth your distinctive qualities—the shining star that resides within you, transcending the confines of our thoughts. This inner gift or calling is an integral part of your identity, and your task is to convey it fervently to people all over the world.

You take something that others thought was worthless elsewhere and transform it into a magnificent creation that everyone can admire. The world might have rejected you countless times, but the artist within you has the ability to rescue a star that humanity has discarded, breathe new life into it, and make it gleam brightly for the entire world to behold.

You might have experienced failure in every journey you embarked upon, attempting to open every door you encountered. Nevertheless, you cannot be defined by these failures; they do not determine your worth. Instead, you should embrace and cherish your true self, loving every aspect of who you are. Your dedication to various commitments in life and business may have left little room for self-appreciation. However, if you embark on a quest to discover the unique qualities within you, you will unearth your essence. Through this journey, you will not only learn to value yourself but also recognize your significance in the broader world that surrounds you.

Even though someone may have strong preferences, what defines a talented artist or captivates someone's heart regarding our identity or another person's identity? It's something that resonates with everyone, allowing us all to connect and empathize or find common ground. Any well-told story possesses the power to reach a broad audience. However, we cannot overlook the truth that we can all sometimes become conceited or excessively proud of our journey from humble beginnings to our current status. This transformation can provide something relatable and motivational for anyone to comprehend.

The vast realm of knowledge can sometimes prove challenging for individuals who strive to gain a deeper understanding of life. It's not always possible to find complete contentment with the person you have evolved into or the trials you encounter during your journey. Every aspect of your identity has the potential to be employed to your disadvantage, irrespective of your financial status, whether you are affluent, prosperous, or struggling financially.

In a vast world where you strive to earn a livelihood by engaging in business endeavors, you might encounter situations where your vulnerabilities could be exposed, potentially leading to the exploitation of your knowledge and skills. However, choosing the path of an artist sets you apart in a distinctive manner. It entails the genuine embrace of your unique individuality and the celebration of the remarkable gift you've nurtured. Every artistic endeavor we embark upon has the remarkable power to awaken and cultivate the deep reservoir of love that resides within us as human beings.

You can't always reach the exact spot where you feel truly important or appreciated for everything you are. Instead, what you often encounter is a constantly changing world that tirelessly attempts to reveal individuals' shortcomings. Your efforts may not always meet the expectations. Therefore, our aim should be to endeavor to attain the part of us that is creative and contributes meaning to all our actions. If you ever feel lost or desire something unique within yourself, you'll be astonished by what you discover as you embark on the journey to explore your inner self.

Within you, there lies an incredible gift that truly defines your essence. This unique gift enables you to communicate effectively with the entire world. Even when you may feel disoriented or uncertain, embracing this inner gift leads you to discover a profound love for all that exists in the world. It's just that sometimes, when we wholeheartedly commit to pursuing something we deeply desire, we become less inclined to consider other available options.

Sometimes, we tend to fall into stereotypes as we pursue our goals. We can become narrow-minded, unwilling to explore the possibilities beyond our current understanding. It's essential to avoid constraining your mental abilities by confining yourself to preconceived notions. Instead, consider exploring the potential within you, which can open up opportunities for personal growth and a greater capacity to love in everything you do.

Sometimes, there may come moments when you must be willing to explore the depths of your heart and consider alternative routes when a straightforward path to success is not evident. Permit the power of art to help you reconnect with your true purpose, enabling you to contribute something authentic. You might be a young individual who has dedicated themselves to a pursuit that hasn't yielded any rewards, causing you to continually lose yourself in the process. You have a profound awareness that this cycle won't come to an end; it will persistently deplete your essence until there's nothing left to offer. Nonetheless, you have the potential to discover a new realm that demands nothing from you, a realm that wholeheartedly embraces your unique identity.

It continues to provide you with what you rightfully deserve, even though we often bestow upon ourselves an excess that makes it challenging to retrace our steps. Nevertheless, you are aware of the places where you haven't misplaced anything valuable. Now, what you might require is to firmly grasp onto that realm and steadily advance within it, even when numerous forces attempt to pull you back into a lifestyle that drains your vitality. Persevere and carry on.

When you wish to leave a lasting impact, it's important to be true to yourself, explore your own special narrative, and share it in a way that conveys your affection for the world and its inhabitants. By doing this, you can recognize your distinct abilities and the wealth of knowledge you were born with. It's time to demonstrate to yourself that you can accomplish great things with the talents you possess, all while staying authentic to your true self.

You will never truly lose your way, for sometimes, you might question the significance of your life; nevertheless, this could mark the inception of a fresh and transformative epoch. It's not merely the narrative itself that molds someone into a skilled artist, but rather the art of articulating it in a manner that resonates with a broader audience, enabling them to grasp your perspective. When you discern the unique qualities within yourself and concentrate on them, you'll gain greater insight into the art of establishing effective connections with people from all walks of life.

You may not always have the perfect story to share with someone or to tell the world about. Sometimes, you might feel a bit lost in the vastness of life, searching for your true self, and wondering if you truly matter amidst everything. It can be a bit confusing, can't it? That feeling of not being able to connect with your inner self and care about who you are.

But, don't worry; you don't have to search too hard. Just take a deep breath and look within, and you'll discover your amazing self. You'll find that you're a unique individual, and everyone will come to appreciate the wonderful person you are, as you're an integral part of the universe.

Every person has two aspects within them. One of these aspects has been with you since childhood. If you don't maintain proper discipline, you won't achieve success when approaching the world from this perspective. It's as if everyone has observed this part of you. To succeed through this aspect of your identity, you must cultivate a particular discipline that reflects positively on who you are. This way, you can rediscover a deeper sense of your inner self and potentially create a livelihood from it.

The other part of our identity emerges when everything we've tried has not succeeded. It's not precisely the same gentle aspect of ourselves that we were born with, directed towards life. Each person possesses this element within them, and it concentrates on a distinct facet of our being. If explored thoroughly, it has the potential to astonish us with the depths of our capabilities through our self-awareness.

If you have maintained discipline since birth, you can maximize your life's potential, which is something everyone is aware of and relies on. You can excel on the common path that we all take, typically through our educational journey. This is just one of the many avenues available to us, and within this route, endeavor to maintain a strong focus.

If you aim to face reality from this perspective, you should have already given your best effort to stand out. The challenge lies in the uncertainty of knowing the precise way to excel and leave a lasting impression on the world, especially if you lack discipline. It's possible to bypass the principles of discipline that all humans adhere to by immersing yourself in the new version of yourself, which exists within every individual. Try to astonish the world with your unique character. When the person you were since birth becomes weary of handling things from this viewpoint, which is the conventional way to confront reality, it's time to formulate a fresh strategy.

Finding a good plan might not always be easy. When you've exhausted all your choices, it can be a challenge to locate something truly significant about your identity. However, don't lose hope. You can tap into the love within you, a genuine love that encompasses everything in existence. This profound affection is what art can harness to manifest your creative essence into the physical world.

As you delve deeper, you'll encounter a profound connection with yourself, where your passion for this world burns brightly. Even though it may initially seem challenging to fathom or accept, there is a wealth of hidden potential within each of us. Unraveling the true narrative of our own lives is a journey that we often don't embark on.

We often face judgment for our actions, even when we don't realize that these actions could lead to discrimination against us. Our chances of navigating through life successfully become quite slim due to our heavy reliance on a crucial aspect—the corporate ladder we aspire to ascend and maintain our position at the pinnacle.

If you wish to gain a profound understanding of matters or successfully reach your objectives, you need to demonstrate unwavering commitment to your chosen path. Our collective endeavor extends far beyond borders as we relentlessly pursue excellence in our respective domains. It's entirely plausible that you may have never delved as deeply into the realms of knowledge enhancement and discipline. Consequently, throughout your lifetime, you may have missed opportunities that remained concealed elsewhere.

Sometimes, we can't see the path ahead clearly. When we try to move forward, we realize that the road we want to take is entirely blocked, and there's no way for us to reach our goals. We encounter three levels of challenges: the traditional path, which demands strict discipline and unwavering focus from an early age. Alternatively, you might have to adopt someone else's perspective or carve your own path through your accumulated knowledge to reach the realm of successful individuals on the other side.

Many times, when you keep facing repeated failures in your journey through life, you might start wondering what could be going wrong. Even if you're confident that you've put forth your utmost effort to achieve something positive, it can be perplexing. You could have completed all the necessary tasks, only to realize that success remains elusive. Perhaps you understood the importance of staying focused on your responsibilities in various situations, yet you failed to incorporate discipline into the execution of your duties. Consequently, you find yourself lagging behind in many aspects of your life. It's possible that there's a significant element on the path to success, one that involves avoiding wrongdoing, refraining from committing crimes, and not harming or offending others.

We must maintain our focus diligently. By doing so, you can achieve your aspirations and ascend to the heights of success that have always occupied your dreams. Imagine a meticulous system that thoroughly examines every aspect of your existence. Ignoring it and feigning obliviousness to the scrutiny of the world is not an option. The world has indeed borne witness to your transgressions. It's unnecessary to operate in the daylight or conceal your actions under the cover of darkness while engaging in illicit deeds that we've all been a part of. Someone or something is scrutinizing our actions closely. The fact is, we all rely on this oversight, and if I happen to spot your error today, it might be my turn tomorrow to seize an opportunity where you faltered.

The world can be quite harsh when you don't grasp what's needed, and if you can't guide yourself positively, failure might keep tracking you wherever you go. You might linger in uncertainty, pondering why things went wrong, as something might have gone awry for failure to occur. Perhaps, the universe intended us to be disciplined, and if we haven't acted appropriately, what awaits those who've displayed respect for life?

As you progress in life and encounter various challenges, you may start to grasp the underlying causes behind your lack of productivity. Nevertheless, there exists an opportunity to reconnect with reality and unlock your maximum potential, although this journey may not follow conventional paths. While the support and comprehension of others may have aided your survival, it may not have fully unleashed your true potential. Therefore, if you have faith in yourself and nurture it, you can embark on a personal quest to unearth a unique pathway to success that resides deep within you, crafted through your distinct thought processes and perspectives.

You can practice self-honesty by taking a moment to reflect on where you may have encountered challenges. When you find yourself in a seemingly insurmountable situation, you will come to a profound realization: your existence holds great significance, and you possess the capability to overcome obstacles and attain extraordinary achievements independently. You will come to understand that there are no mountains too tall for you to conquer. Even if you've faced failures in your past endeavors, your intellectual comprehension will guide you out of any circumstance.

Having ample motivation alone may not suffice to attain your desired outcomes through creation. You must actively pave your unique path forward. Otherwise, you might endure a prolonged period of fruitless contemplation, navigating the obscurities within your own psyche, unable to discern your precise location. Your knowledge and skills could be present, but they may seem misplaced within this world, not serving their intended purpose or making meaningful connections. You may falter in your pursuit of these goals.

When you're supposed to be on track with your discipline, but you veer away from it, your life starts moving towards the future version of yourself. If you don't behave well, you won't be able to achieve your goals. You'll never reach the point where your dreams can come true, and whatever you're aiming for will seem impossible to attain. It might feel like nothing is going your way. However, through the power of the arts, you can find the person who got lost in the depths of your own knowledge.

You might have faced harsh judgment because of who you are, but deep down, you realize that things shouldn't always be this way. The truth is, you can emerge from this situation, and you should never carry guilt with you forever. There is a place somewhere where you can rediscover your innocence, free from all the accusations the world has thrown at you.

When the world has turned against you, and you find yourself far from your desired destination, you may come to the realization that despite your initial intentions to do good, you've somehow strayed from the path you were meant to follow. Many times, our failures can be traced back to the small missteps of our youth. As you reflect on these minor errors, you begin to notice that your life has shifted from its previous course. The challenging part is that you often don't recognize these deviations early on; you continue down an uncertain path without understanding why it has led to such bitterness.

You can imagine many things happening without fully grasping the essence of life or love. Achieving these concepts can pose a significant challenge because we sometimes make mistakes in both situations. When it comes to relationships, our actions can not only impact our own lives but also have far-reaching effects on everything we are. To address these challenges, you may need to discover your inner artistry. The artistic aspect within us serves as a conduit to realign our humanity with its true purpose.

Even if you've made mistakes throughout your entire life, there's a remark-able power within you. When you harness this power, you can connect with your inner self—a person seeking a place in the world, yearning for acceptance just as they are. Your creative work and understanding allow you to express your true self, especially in situations where you've faltered or recognized your errors. Moreover, this process enables you to carefully shape your entire being back to its core essence.

You have the opportunity to transform the way people perceive you, and you can rejuvenate yourself in various aspects of life and love by connecting with your inner self. You start being truthful with the person you've evolved into, and you take a moment to introspect, examining your soul's reflection to iden-tify where you may have made missteps thus far.

When something in your life goes wrong and can't be fixed, you might won-der who or what you can count on. Who deserves your loyalty? Who can you trust? Can you have faith in yourself? Yes, you can have confidence in who you are. You can take the time to focus on what's important and see yourself returning to reality. You can discover someone with limitless abilities who can transform any situation into something beautiful.

Sometimes, there might be instances when you lose sight of your true self. You see, each of us is born with an inherent potential that defines our essence. However, it's quite common for us to inadvertently undermine our opportuni-ties for success. We may unknowingly veer down a wayward path, making poor choices and failing to perceive things correctly from the outset. In such mo-ments, it becomes imperative to seek a means to rediscover your significance as a valuable individual.

When you make mistakes and don't do things correctly, it can affect every part of you. After a while, you might see your life falling apart. But if you discover the goodness inside you, you won't experience suffering. Everything you've ever wished for since you were born, the world gives to you without asking. Our lack of understanding can cause a lot of harm, and sometimes we don't even notice when the path ahead is clear.

When you reach a point where you can't recognize yourself anymore due to feeling lost and despondent, there's still a way to rediscover and rebuild yourself. You have the power to reshape your entire existence in alignment with your unique comprehension. Although we can never fully recreate our original selves from birth, by dedicating your complete focus, faith, and love to the process, you can unearth the hidden depths of your soul and draw out the untapped greatness within you that you might never have known existed.

Through the power of art, you can reconnect with your inner self, becoming the sole arbiter of your life's choices, including those errors you may have made. Even though we face consequences for our past transgressions, there is an opportunity to rectify them, though the effort may demand a toll on your overall well-being. In the wake of lost love, you can rekindle your genuine sense of dedication. When the blessings of life slip through your grasp, you have the chance to unearth a renewed self, one tailored for the journey you're embarking upon.

Deep within you, there's a great potential for understanding life in its entirety. You possess the power to create extraordinary things even in unexpected places. When life loses its meaning, you can find a new purpose. From the wounds within your soul, you can heal and transform yourself. Instead of dwelling on others' mistakes, you focus on your own, tirelessly striving to correct every fault and error you've accumulated. We are born with certain patterns we shouldn't disrupt in our lives. Changing them makes us less aligned with creation.

To successfully overcome any setback that comes your way, it's crucial to stay true to your original self as you were when you were born. If you alter your core essence from what it once was, you may start to amass vulnerabilities. While these setbacks won't permanently depart from your life, they will persist, causing you to vanish amidst the disappointments that infiltrate all your endeavors. To reverse this trend, you must delve deep into your inner self and commence the process of rectifying those errors.

You transform yourself into a work of art, crafting a fresh portrayal of your identity and your emotions. This dedication to self-examination is where we discover ourselves when we seem to have lost our way. Embracing your inner artist can reshape you into a new version of yourself, one you may have never before glimpsed or comprehended in your life journey. When adversity tests our very essence, seek the love that resides within, a force yearning to manifest itself in the real world.

Art is like a hidden piece of ourselves that waits patiently for the perfect moment to emerge. It's when you nurture and shape it into something extraordinary. Even when everything seems to be working against you, there lies your genuine inner spirit, yearning for connection with the world. You may have experienced losses in the past, but now is your opportunity to reclaim everything you rightly deserve.

Having a passion for art deep within, it's time to seize a fresh opportunity that has come your way. Ensure that you make the most of this chance that has been bestowed upon you to become a meaningful creator. It's truly unfortunate that in the lives we've been granted, everything comes with a set of rules that should not be ignored. Failing to adhere to these life and love guidelines has now made us confront the harsh realities of our choices.

As humans, we tend to take advantage of opportunities we come across. It's in our nature. But, if you've done something good, don't just stop at that. Keep going, don't stop anytime soon. Keep doing good things until you've reached a point where your whole life is defined by your positive actions. You keep evolving as a person, nurturing the beliefs you've developed, and steadily turning them into a masterpiece of creativity.

Once you've discovered who you truly are and what your purpose entails, don't halt your journey. Instead, persevere, and in doing so, you'll come to recognize that the world isn't inherently malevolent; rather, our failure often lies in our inability to grasp what's expected of us. Nevertheless, if you possess the capacity, refrain from fixating on others' lives and concentrate on your personal comprehension. Keep learning until everything becomes clear. The key is that if your pursuit never attains the pinnacle of creative formation, your success may remain elusive.

You have the power to transform the challenges in your life into something truly remarkable, a splendid expression of your unique self. This incredible capability resides within you, but sometimes people fail to recognize how to harness it effectively. From the moment we are born, we possess an innate potential for greatness. However, the temptations of this world often lead us astray, causing us to make irreversible mistakes. Yet, through the practice of art, we rediscover our inner purity and reconnect with our authentic selves, enabling us to reclaim all that we are meant to be.

We can engage in artistic endeavors to cleanse and refine our inner selves. By fostering unwavering determination in both our actions and character, art has played a pivotal role in giving rise to the individual you have become during your earthly existence. It has extended its forgiveness to absolve you of past transgressions. What has perished is the persona you carried from your very birth. Can we distinguish between the various types of wrongs we commit? Are there any actions you can undertake that bear no consequences, or do certain grave offenses automatically lead to consequences? So, what is the final judgment? When it comes to our collective wrongdoing, who bears the greater burden of punishment?

Each action you take has an effect on the outcomes you'll achieve. Throughout your lifetime, you might face challenges while searching for the perfect companion, but remember, you possess the power to unlock that unique person's heart. By making positive changes and excelling, you can carve out a meaningful role in their life. As we begin, let's recite the following prayer:

'Our Father, who resides in heaven...'

Chapter Eleven

The Heart of a Child

You might be one of those individuals who have experienced both love and its ups and downs without altering themselves. When the time comes to commit once more, you carry on loving as you always have. One thing you must watch out for is how fixated the world can become with someone's life. Some individuals might insist you follow their lead and their pursuits, especially when you've just uncovered something extraordinary and unique about your own existence. Many people may attempt to discourage you from residing in your own world, which you've labored diligently to construct through your own comprehension. This can sometimes make you feel as though there's no reason to persevere.

You will encounter people who expect you to stay true to their beliefs, even if you work hard to explain the purpose, objectives, and inspiration behind your creation or concept. It might seem like an ongoing struggle where you can't seem to gain their understanding. It can feel like an unending battle to uphold your convictions deep within your being. Eventually, you come to understand that forging your own path is a challenging endeavor.

As a person striving to accomplish something special in your life, you may wonder, "What is the main reason for taking part in your various endeavors?"

Do you persist in your pursuits because you believe there is a great deal you comprehend about life, or do you continue onward because you are dedicated to a particular concept that has become more significant to you than anything else in your life?

In the journey of invention, you'll encounter numerous challenges and obstacles along the way. However, it's crucial never to let doubt creep into your mind. If your goal is to strive for greatness, you must maintain unwavering belief in your ideas. Dedicate yourself wholeheartedly to the tasks at hand, even in the face of negativity from others regarding your aspirations. Remember that you've recognized the value within yourself, and your self-love is so profound that you'll never forsake your quest and the dreams you hold dear.

Sometimes, your understanding can face deep challenges due to everything around you.

However, if you truly believe in what you're doing, don't just do it once and then switch to something else. Dedicate yourself to it for the long haul, and you will notice your faith guiding you along a clear path in life. Make it a fundamental part of the journey you've chosen to embark on indefinitely. Don't ever look back and feel like you no longer matter in the situation, as people might try to divert you from your path. Give it your all and ensure you've done everything necessary so that you don't become the one who fails humanity. Instead, let the world disappoint you if need be, but fulfill your responsibilities as you should.

Allow the goal of keeping a promise to be entrusted to the other person; this is a wise choice in any circumstance. Once you have completed your responsibilities, take a moment to relax and forgive any misunderstandings that may have arisen along the journey. Concentrate on what truly matters in life, which is discovering a special someone who can hold a special place in your heart. Someone who loves you deeply and fills the void that arises from neglecting commitment.

As you journey through life, you'll encounter moments when you might feel unsure about what you're doing because you haven't reached your destination yet. However, deep down, you possess the knowledge and skills needed to confidently navigate every challenge that lies ahead. It's important not to be too hard on yourself for embarking on a significant and one-of-a-kind endeavor, even if you haven't seen immediate benefits. Consider it as the unique path you've chosen for yourself, and remain steadfast, knowing that you wouldn't alter your course, no matter what unfolds.

You don't need to call it a situation in which you couldn't succeed with "the invention" and spoil your chances of success as you had hoped. We come from a world where you must realize that discovering yourself, understanding what you're doing, is essential to be the only person sufficient for all tasks. It's important to meet the requirement of adequacy, as not everything out there is meant to shape the world; individuals can repurpose things that have failed in various situations and incorporate them into the creative process. Even though they understand it may not work for everyone, failing to grasp our ideas or inventions can allow failure to have a negative impact on people's lives.

Some individuals may have had various choices available to them, whereas others might not possess any alternatives regarding the individuals they interact with. Instead, they have embarked on a singular path that they've uncovered for themselves, one that involves manifesting their dreams into reality. Consequently, it becomes challenging to channel one's productivity into other creative pursuits, as life predominantly revolves around their chosen path. Thus, if you're unable to sustain a livelihood from your chosen idea, regardless of its potential strength, repercussions will inevitably emerge. This is because you'll struggle to fulfill all the responsibilities that come with being a self-sustaining individual.

In all the activities we immerse ourselves in, something important must be sacrificed, whether it's our time, personal space, affection, existence, or whatever is necessary for the other side of our identity to discover its full self. To venture beyond the standard realm of comprehension and acquaint oneself with this world typically requires something essential for ordinary functioning.

As we embark on our individual journeys, many people may initially assume that you are pursuing a similar path to theirs. However, you persist in following the unique life path you've forged for yourself. By doing so, you have the potential to establish a distinctive presence and embody a novel concept or notion that remains unexplored. You can even transcend rivalry by immersing yourself in a realm that cannot rival your distinctive essence. This is achievable by centering your attention on self-development and embracing your distinctiveness. You stand resolute in the knowledge that you personify an entirely distinctive and unparalleled concept.

Can we engage in competition by utilizing our expertise and wealth of experience, or by leveraging our profound comprehension and mastery of the precise methods necessary for achieving success? Moreover, as you approach the culmination of your endeavors, it is imperative to ensure that you have diligently adhered to these principles to achieve triumphant outcomes. It's essential to recognize that every obstacle encountered during your journey serves as a stepping stone towards the realization of your aspirations, molding you into the individual you aspire to become. One should not allow external pressures to cast doubt upon their self-worth, for it is imperative to acknowledge your intrinsic value. While there may exist domains in your life where you may not possess a high degree of competence, you can always excel in comprehending the intricacies of your pursuits. Your reservoir of knowledge should serve as a guiding force, constantly grounding you in the realm of reality when faced with challenges.

You can't know everything, but don't let that discourage you. Stay motivated because when you make a breakthrough, it will greatly impact your success. Your commitment to standing out may weaken your focus on a regular life, as you can't do both simultaneously. However, in the end, it will transform you and empower you to overcome challenges that used to bring you down.

When you are really motivated to become highly skilled in your job, even if it requires you to do more than your usual tasks. When things haven't gone well for you, and even though you can't always forget about it, because even when you've tried your best to learn more about your field, there will still be challenges ahead.

Examinations regarding the merits of competence become relevant when one's talent has been likened or mirrored. After this, the subsequent step involves mirroring these innovative qualities. These qualities serve as gateways to completeness, enabling one to perceive illumination. When these qualities are utilized in a suitable manner, they stand ready to adorn our endeavors with success. Irrespective of the difficulties encountered in any given situation, it becomes imperative to apply each of these qualities meticulously. By doing so, you are poised to witness triumph throughout your entire journey. These qualities manifest in every facet of our activities, and by comprehending their correct application, you can traverse a considerable distance along your path to self-improvement.

It might be a situation where you've dedicated yourself to something that will impact many lives. You should aspire to return with added value, as vanishing indefinitely isn't an option. You'll experience a reawakening in all the areas where you've wholeheartedly dedicated your life.

Even when something doesn't work out as planned, you can make it successful by using the qualities of creativity. For example, having patience in all your endeavors, staying composed and relaxed, and avoiding unnecessary actions when facing challenges can help protect you from current difficulties. This approach may ultimately rescue you from tough situations, as your understanding of a situation can evolve over time, influenced by the experience gained through your efforts.

Some people might struggle to exercise patience when it's essential. This impatience can hinder their chances of success. Failing to harness the full spectrum of creative virtues could lead to disappointment. In life, success often depends on mastering various virtues. Patience, alongside other qualities, is a key ingredient in achieving your goals. By cultivating these virtues, you increase your likelihood of prospering in all your endeavors. In everything you undertake, you receive rewards when you exhibit patience and embrace the other virtues of life. Through this approach, you successfully complete the tasks assigned to you.

Sometimes, you might believe you've achieved victory in the war, but in reality, the true struggle has yet to commence. Challenges arrive and depart intermittently. However, if you have found inner harmony with yourself and every endeavor you undertake, you will grasp that much of what unfolds along your journey contributes to the shaping of your life. When you engage with the entirety of creation, novel circumstances continuously surface, and it becomes impossible to possess complete knowledge of them all.

In life, there's a part where you'll recognize your achievements, and there's also a part where you'll admit your shortcomings. When you reflect on your failures, it can sometimes lead to negative self-feelings, which might hinder your progress in life. The previous version of ourselves, which we're probably leaving behind, is where we didn't excel in certain areas. Even though we're making progress in the new phase of our lives, it's important to remain watchful and attentive.

You should strive to grasp things with precision because there might be instances where your competence isn't put to proper use, and this can create an impression of incompetence. Therefore, it's important to accept your current state and recognize that knowledge can provide temporary freedom.

Have a kind and compassionate heart that is dedicated to making a positive impact. When your heart is filled with goodness, you'll have the chance to see how your actions can transform the world and contribute to its improvement. The kindness within your heart will not only fulfill your deepest desires but will also touch the lives of those you encounter. Always believe in your abilities and knowledge; they will prove to be sufficient for all your needs. In time, you will apply your many qualities effectively and make a meaningful difference in the world.

Develop a strong passion for learning and gaining a deep understanding of what it means to be a creative genius. There are moments in life when we are called upon to possess extensive knowledge about everything we engage in. It's during these times when you must be well-informed about the challenges you encounter, to the extent that you may feel overwhelmed by the circumstances. However, even during these frustrating periods in our lives that make forgiveness seem difficult, strive to maintain a positive outlook and continue contributing to the betterment of the world.

Your reactions to situations that bring sadness can reveal a great deal about your character. At times, you may experience a strong desire for prolonged resentment, extending far beyond the possibility of forgiveness. This may occur when you observe the reckless actions of many individuals who aim to hinder others from advancing in their life journeys.

We all have imperfections, and we've faced various challenges on our journey to reach our current state. Sometimes, when we encounter people whose actions baffle us, anger can alter our perspective. It's important to remember that every person possesses the potential for both kindness and harm within their hearts, but whether those darker emotions take hold depends on your choices. So, it's worth considering whether you should let the emotions brewing within you transform into hatred or simply integrate them into your daily experiences.

It's important to remember that you do matter, just like everyone else. The key is not to get upset when things don't go as planned. When you've done your best and things still aren't going well, it's best to be patient and wait for the right moment. Eventually, you'll see that your desires can become reality as you journey towards your goals.

Sometimes, you might encounter individuals who don't comprehend your actions to the extent that they are willing to witness your destruction. However, you can choose to pardon that aspect as well and establish harmony with all that exists. Much of what we feel about the world holds true, but as we engage in the process of creation, reality undergoes transformations, and elements gradually fall into their rightful places, aligning precisely with their destined roles. The pursuit of something elusive without a clear path to attain it is futile. Instead, persisting in your endeavors will unveil that much of it aligns with your initial perception.

Your life truly does matter, but it's important to remember that you don't need to harm anyone as you strive to reach the place you aspire to be. There may be moments when you believe you are fully prepared for the world and understand what is expected of you, but sometimes, that might not be the case. While you're on that journey, it's possible to be mistaken about many things, and anyone can find themselves in such a situation.

Many people find themselves daydreaming about a life they wish they had, even though they may not have a clear path to achieve their desired goals. Sometimes, we pursue our dreams with such intensity that we disregard the necessary steps to reach them. This can lead us to make sacrifices that are not in our best interest. However, it's important to recognize the value of understanding what you're doing. This understanding can have a healing effect on us as human beings. It allows us to grasp the significance of our actions and refrain from insisting on having things our way when we are unsure of how to attain our dreams.

Creating things is beautiful because we can tell when something is just right. We strive to do our very best to accomplish something truly worthwhile. When we do it with precision, adhering to the exact way it must be done, we often find ourselves in situations where we have important goals to achieve, and we work hard to achieve them in the best way possible.

Discovering the precise way to do things marks an initial step on your journey to creativity. You've already achieved this milestone, but there's still more to learn and master. Remember, you've had a breakthrough, but you're not yet an expert at attracting everything you desire through your newfound knowledge. It's crucial not to overlook the importance of love in this process; without it, something significant is missing from your path, which you may not fully grasp at the moment. Your new path holds potential, but you need a deeper understanding to navigate it successfully.

How can you be sure that your actions are correct? Sometimes, you aren't even provided with assurance that your endeavors are on the right path. Nonetheless, it's important to recognize that life often feels like a journey with uncertain outcomes. Many challenges lie ahead in your pursuit of whatever you desire, and it's essential to maintain your belief in yourself. Furthermore, if you're relatively new to this world, you may feel like you lack knowledge about the complexities of the world. In such a situation, you primarily rely on your own understanding, and as time passes, you may gradually realize how much you still have to learn.

Everything you're doing is correct, just as it should be. However, you're pursuing it from a different perspective on life. Despite your earnest efforts, your lack of experience has become evident too soon. Consequently, you may find it challenging to attain your desired achievements or success in the way you envision. This leads you to struggle to establish a foundation for your unique perspective. Throughout your life, you've held the belief that your approach is effective, but the world often fails to see things from your viewpoint. They seek alterations in your actions or the outcomes of your objectives. Ultimately, you must persevere to maintain your steadfast belief and not deviate from your objectives.

Facing tough and sad situations is a common part of life. These challenging moments test us until we find something dependable to rely on. For someone to misjudge you, the world has to put its own well-being at risk. It's like grasping onto a pillar to build a path towards success. When you do this, you realize that this path is just, and there's a place for everyone with something valuable to offer. You truly grasp this when you've overcome your personal struggles to become who you truly want to be.

Once you attain such a high level of achievement, you become unstoppable. You're not only free to express your ideas but also embark on a thrilling journey of creativity. You firmly hold the belief that justice will eventually prevail for all the hard work you've put in, and indeed, it does, irrespective of the time it may take, resulting in your well-deserved recognition.

Being young can feel incredibly thrilling because you're eager to explore the world. However, when something existed before, everything can become quite different. Don't blame creation for not understanding where it's headed. Many people can find happiness in life just the way it is. If you continue to do things your way, you might attract someone who needs your help. Your efforts will persist, and eventually, the door of creativity could open, allowing you to discover your place within it. If you can't stand opposition or settling for second place, then aim to excel in everything you do and put in the effort to secure the top position.

Becoming the finest in your chosen profession is quite challenging. It necessitates a significant amount of effort and dedication. This is because the world's operations can be quite complex and unpredictable. Once you attain such a high level of expertise, it's crucial to recognize that your actions and decisions can have a far-reaching impact on various aspects of the world around you. Although it's impossible to fully comprehend all the factors that have contributed to the current state of affairs, especially when you're still young, you possess the ability to shape your own personal universe and strive to bring about positive change.

To ensure you avoid engaging in wrongdoing, it's essential to position yourself as the utmost dependable individual globally. Strive to gain acceptance from all things and individuals, as everyone craves positivity in their existence. Eventually, you may find yourself as the sole possessor of precise knowledge, possibly necessitating your involvement in various systems and assuming responsibility for humanity's well-being.

One crucial aspect to consider is ensuring that you learn how to recognize the effects of your creation on people's lives. You should also be capable of explaining and comprehending the role you envision for yourself in the broader scope of humanity. It's important to clearly articulate the purpose and functionality of your innovation, as well as how it will make a positive difference in society. Additionally, consider where your invention might be valuable on a global scale.

Do you envision your idea being embraced and utilized by a specific community? Perhaps you aspire to have your concept embraced on a global scale, spanning every corner of the world. Are you prepared to coexist with individuals who hold differing viewpoints? It's crucial to remember that you are not alone on the global stage, and truly original ideas are quite rare.

You simply want to provide a superior method compared to other inventors. Some of these inventors might have come up with older ideas that offer similar solutions but fall short in various aspects. In such instances, you have identified a chance to step in and enhance that aspect of life, making incremental improvements. You can present yourself as an expert in the worldwide marketplace, offering the finest service among all the options out there.

If you truly desire a comprehensive understanding, it's crucial to recognize a fundamental truth about people: they are incredibly diverse and distinct in all aspects of their lives. People represent a wide spectrum of humanity, each possessing unique qualities and leading varied lifestyles. Sometimes, you may need to set aside your preconceived notions and prioritize your interactions with individuals, even when it may seem unnecessary.

You continue to have faith in the idea that defines your entire existence, except now you've reached a higher level, reflecting your profound concern for humanity. You've transitioned to an entirely new stage where you strive to be the finest version of yourself. You treat everyone with equality, making room for every individual in the world. It's in this situation that you might encounter a dilemma, as you won't be the one to utilize your own invention.

You are the creator of various objects and concepts. Your ideas might seem straightforward to you, but for individuals encountering them for the first time, how should they incorporate these ideas into their own lives? Furthermore, as you accumulate knowledge about human beings, you ultimately must reconcile and find harmony with the wealth of insights you've gained.

Up to this point, if the world hasn't yet astonished you, rest assured that you'll be truly amazed by the prospect of becoming a widely recognized and utilized brand by people from all walks of life. Regardless of their economic status, individuals will undoubtedly discover that their requirements are attended to. It's only when you've executed your tasks meticulously that you'll be capable of accommodating everyone's diverse needs. It won't be a mere affirmative response; rather, you should always bear in mind that your offerings must seamlessly integrate into people's daily lives.

How much are people aware of the idea you want to make happen? Does it change depending on how old they are? Is it something that's for everyone, from babies to elderly folks? When you don't understand this, it feels like the world has turned into a big mountain you're trying to climb. Just making a living becomes really hard. It might not be simple, but if you discover that special place, that grip, that thing that makes everything work perfectly, it can make all your dreams come true, just like they should. Don't let anything change your mind. Everything you've been thinking about could eventually come true, even if it takes a lot longer and you've had to endure more pressure than you expected.

When you didn't understand, you saw your own invention as an enemy. But when you gained knowledge of what you were doing, it became easier for you to work with everything. Now, let's consider how to mend the effects that time can have on your life, especially now that you've reached the stage of manifesting your projects. The anger you hold within yourself might make you feel emotionally drained. Nevertheless, if you possess a forgiving heart capable of letting go of all you've experienced, you can ultimately discover a sense of peace amidst all your endeavors.

Everything might turn out fine in the end, but not having enough experience might have made it impossible for you to see the future with everything you're doing. Therefore, it's important to always keep kindness in your heart and show that you care about others. This can make a big difference because if you focus only on yourself, you might accidentally mess up something that could have turned out great. Remember, you can't see everything all at once, ideas develop as you go along, and your life could start to make more sense as you move forward.

By the close of the day, as you gain knowledge in treating others kindly, even when encountering those who may not have initially wished you success due to your lack of experience, you might discover the potential for remarkable achievements. It's possible that your initial hopes could falter, but numerous unexpected opportunities may arise, including those you never anticipated. Remember, expertise doesn't emerge overnight; it develops over time as we gain more experience.

Have a generous heart that can embrace a lot of people. If you're not sure where to find that kind and humble person, take a moment to explore deep within your own soul. When you do, you'll uncover a person of inner strength, someone truly worth having in your life to make it more enjoyable. Don't allow the person you used to be to fade away; instead, hold onto that version of yourself with all your might. By doing so, you can uncover your true self, someone who listens and comprehends everything you do, and this can lead to a place where others no longer engage in conflicts with you.

One important point to remember is that you haven't lost anything when you take action, even if you spend a long time grappling with uncertainty in pursuit of success. Your life maintains its inherent value from the very start. Through this journey, you've gained valuable insights about the world, even if tangible results are scarce. It's true that anyone can potentially cause harm to others, but that shouldn't undermine your purpose, as some may have regarded you in a different light.

Whenever you engage in any task or activity, remember that if you place love at its core, you have the ability to return to it if you encounter challenges along the way. Love is the key to leading a fulfilling life. It's essential to recognize that people possess an innate sense of understanding. It's best not to harm them when they mean no harm to you. Additionally, you can gain valuable insights by allowing yourself to be vulnerable temporarily. However, if you maintain your focus and exhibit patience during this process, you will ultimately achieve a truly remarkable life.

The more time you spend doing something, the easier it gets. When you're near the finish line, tasks that initially seemed like they'd take forever become effortless. Don't let anyone's attempts to hold you back deter you; you'll start with less and end up with just as much as you hadn't expected. The weight of your responsibilities lightens as you progress, and you'll eventually reach a point where many of the challenges you once found daunting will appear straightforward.

Studying is truly beneficial. If you maintain your belief in the power of education and consistently apply yourself to the task, you can undoubtedly attain greatness. The solutions to all the challenges you face in life can be discovered within the framework of your studies. Avoid underestimating yourself and diminishing the value of your efforts. Understand that various factors may attempt to undermine your progress, but by remaining dedicated to becoming the best version of yourself, you can ultimately overcome the negative mindset that seeks to exploit others.

Everything lies along the journey we've embarked upon, as we navigate the early stages of life, striving to extract the utmost from this world. Even the solutions to the most challenging equations can be found on this path, so long as you refrain from inactivity and maintain a serene disposition. Engage in daily introspection, both during daylight and in the quiet of night. Maintain unwavering concentration on your objectives and refrain from evading the truths of existence. Life is a gift, regardless of the seemingly insurmountable circumstances; you will glean valuable insights from your unwavering dedication to your chosen pursuits.

You're never too late when you're striving to complete tasks correctly and on time. It's crucial to release any self-doubt or negative thoughts that may harm your progress. Embracing a youthful, innocent, and fearless mindset can help you tackle challenging tasks. While you may not have all the answers at a young age, having faith in your ability to learn and grow will enable you to mature and gain knowledge as you remain open to learning.

Follow this advice: Put in diligent effort when you're learning until you're able to excel beyond the established norms. Take advantage of opportunities to gain knowledge while they are available; it's crucial to make the most of them. Throughout life, you'll come across both punishments and rewards based on your performance. Failing to grasp concepts thoroughly may push you to explore new horizons. Aim to overcome all challenges and secure a bright future. By doing so, you'll not only save time but also create a prosperous life. Knowledge will serve as the key to fill the void left by misunderstandings.

Chapter Twelve

Woman in Love

There are many things you can teach humans, but teaching them to love each other is not one of them. Loving each other is something they have always known how to do. They know how to stick together and take care of one another. So, as individuals, when we try to understand things, we often lose ourselves in the complexities of relationships because that's what everyone knows best. Sometimes, someone may not fully appreciate someone else, but it doesn't mean people haven't known how to take care of each other. We sometimes wonder why we don't find it easier in our journey of discovery and innovation.

This idea can be applied to many aspects of life, including the things essential for our existence as human beings. Money, too, can have a similar impact on those seeking self-improvement. It's important to keep in mind that you desire recognition, a means to sustain yourself financially, and the satisfaction of others is your goal. Making people happy is your objective, but it may prove challenging to reach the point where they grant you the opportunity to create something meaningful.

As you gaze upon the world, you often ponder why, despite the many years you've spent on the journey of self-discovery, life hasn't always been smooth sailing. Indeed, you may encounter opportunities to enhance your financial prospects. However, there's a stretch of time you must traverse—a period that might prevent you from embracing a contented version of yourself. How can I release something I require, perhaps to appease someone, even if it means sacrificing my own well-being? We often find ourselves adrift when we lack concrete knowledge, and in such moments, we may find ourselves resenting the paths we know deep down aren't in alignment with our true selves.

Being human is fundamentally rooted in our innate understanding of ourselves. It's about how we persevere, regardless of the lessons life imparts. This knowledge forms the bedrock of our existence, serving as our sanctuary and haven, where we find solace and meaning. For me, what unequivocally defines my essence is love and family, making me feel whole and ordinary. Unlike you, who may embrace numerous self-definitions, I find completeness in these simple yet profound aspects of life, and I don't even need to cling to them; they are the very essence of who I am.

Here you are, trying to understand things better and stepping into a specific area where you'll interact with various people. One crucial aspect of your interactions with people is that they value your knowledge and experience. You're there to share what you know and help them become better individuals. However, deep down, we also have our own needs that might have been overlooked, and while some acknowledge that you have needs too, they may not know how to address them, especially when it comes to matters of love.

Relationships shouldn't be troublesome, they should be simple and uncomplicated. However, because of the responsibilities we take on, we sometimes neglect things that are essential for our daily happiness. And the tricky part is, we often struggle to figure out how to recover them. We're constantly tied up with these obligations, and by the time you realize it's time to prioritize what truly matters, you may have lost not only love but also financial stability. This situation might have arisen while you were busy nurturing your ideas. A part of you couldn't fully engage in the workforce to earn a living, causing you to become less effective in those areas due to a lack of focus on those aspects of our lives.

Emerging from such a challenging situation, you may find yourself depending on others to help rediscover your true self. If these people can't be there for you, how do you navigate through the difficulties of life or setbacks on your journey? It's important to recognize that there's a point you must reach where love becomes your primary focus. You desire to be cherished by someone special who values you, particularly as you complete your responsibilities, and relationships become vital.

So, at this juncture where you've lost connection with everything while striving to get everything right, things no longer seem to fall into place as expected. The question arises: do we possess the wisdom and experience needed to reintroduce that essence of love into our lives? Can we once again draw in someone special?

When we find ourselves facing various situations, we often enter them with uncertainty, unsure of what lies ahead. We're driven by the desire to make a difference in the particular aspect that holds significance for us. However, we might not fully grasp the complexity of these situations. As we become engrossed in our ideas and aspirations, we sometimes lose sight of the broader picture. Consequently, we may reach a point where we must address the consequences of time and circumstance, endeavoring to mend what has been negatively affected, even if we're uncertain about the precise path to restoration.

How can you develop deep feelings for someone when you're unsure about their inner thoughts and emotions? It can be a challenging task to embrace a person you barely know, as they reach out to you, seeking affection and a place in your daily existence. This becomes even more complex when the innate inclination to form close bonds seems to have faded, and your very being is molded by a unique wisdom not commonly found among humans.

Your essence undergoes profound transformations. We are inherently inclined to love and lead conventional lives at birth. However, this inclination can sometimes diminish due to our inability to maintain equilibrium. If a scarcity of knowledge were the sole catalyst for love's potential, the world might have descended into chaos. Conversely, an excess of anything isn't the remedy either. At the juncture of complete acceptance by all, an excessive desire for anything becomes undesirable.

If you possess sufficient knowledge, you will stay in your rightful place. However, as our curiosity grows, we may inadvertently lose touch with the essence of life and love. Sometimes, events occur either because of your comprehension or due to your attempts to control them. It's as if the world requires this equilibrium to prevent you from taking complete control of your destiny. Since we lack a comprehensive understanding of what enables everything to exist, our knowledge about our own identity is limited.

What makes us worthy and deserving of all the wonderful opportunities the world presents to us? Perhaps it's because we don't assume to know everything. We continue to rely on various aspects of life, and you don't even have to pray, as long as deep down, your faith in the mighty God remains strong; He will come to your aid and help you succeed. It's a similar concept with everything we strive for in life, and through this equilibrium, we strive to excel and aspire to outshine others in the end.

No matter where you go, even if you couldn't have known a lot in advance, don't expect good luck right from the start. Instead, be ready to work diligently and patiently, pouring your heart and soul into your efforts. Realize that it's not every day that you come across someone who is strong and courageous enough to truly hear your sincere plea for love.

Sometimes, when you feel like you're not getting enough love, it shouldn't catch you off guard. Life has its secrets, and one of them is that delving into certain areas of understanding can make you responsible for your own destiny. It might become quite challenging to comprehend why you face difficulties in your relationships. It's possible that everyone is constantly on the hunt for love, and some may possess the necessary tool to discover it, and that tool is the simplicity of the heart.

You, on the other hand, might have found yourself disconnected from reality when it comes to seeking someone to look after your well-being. Your attention shifted towards seeking answers unrelated to love, and many times, your thoughts weren't aligned with the reality most people embrace. Consequently, you may now realize that you don't currently meet the prerequisites for finding love. This is because, through your own efforts, you haven't reached that point yet. You might liken this situation to someone searching for things they aren't quite ready for, resembling a person pursuing something they don't truly deserve at this moment.

Now, consider how some people are frequently upset, while many others have managed to move ahead in life. You may find yourself unable to take any action because you've lost your direction when it comes to your own thoughts. Moving forward can take one of two paths: you can either diligently put in effort to attain the level of deservingness where life's offerings come naturally, or you can surpass limits by striving to accomplish your goals based on your own comprehension.

Desiring and yearning have always been our innate inclinations toward life, representing our initial endeavors to explore all the opportunities the world presents. Sometimes, we remain unaware that this is precisely where we are meant to be. We dedicate ourselves to numerous pursuits, often losing sight of our true selves. Consequently, the question arises: how can we rediscover our equilibrium and return to a state where our fundamental needs are effortlessly met, eliminating the need for arduous introspection regarding our role in the human experience?

Understanding life can sometimes lead to a dislike for other people. This happens because we often want to do what we want and get more for ourselves. We prefer to see things our way, even though we don't know everything and only know a limited amount. We tend to focus on what we're excited to create, and the part where we have to face reality can be hard to grasp from our perspective.

Many essential aspects of life don't demand rigorous effort to obtain, but comprehending them independently might necessitate acquiring knowledge. How can one attain an education encompassing all the complexities that affect our existence?

Your mind can only grasp a limited amount of knowledge, leaving you to ponder what might have gone awry. Nevertheless, at the forefront, both wealth and affection demand comprehension in their pursuit. They emerge as pivotal prerequisites for human contentment, fostering success and innovation. When you neglect their pursuit, you might suspect external interference hindering your life from finding purpose in this realm.

How can one ensure they comprehend everything essential about the world? Often, we journey through life unaware that our own minds may be the cause of disruptions in our daily existence. When individuals cling to their current state, we might erroneously perceive them as lacking strength to facilitate our desires within the realm of creation. This frustration can lead us to a point where we are uncertain about our course of action, resorting to self-invention devoid of strong moral principles. Yet, the truth remains accessible, though sometimes obscured by our lack of awareness that we have yet to fully embrace it.

You have been putting in effort, but until now, you haven't quite reached the point where you have both love and money. However, if you do reach that point, no one can deny you the opportunity to find happiness. Like everyone else, you desire all that life has to offer. However, you're different from them because you've made the conscious choice to embark on a unique journey to understand your own path. Your destiny is closely tied to your knowledge and understanding.

In the realm of relationships, folks generally prefer not to be taken advantage of. They've known this about themselves for as long as they can remember. People value their entire being, and it's not that they're opposed to change; they simply wish to avoid mistreatment. Deep down, they believe that acquiring things like love and money, without earning them, is unjust.

It's perfectly fine if you're not entirely sure about the exact way to do things. Sometimes, we all crave to attain our goals quickly, and this is a part of life where individuals cannot simply let go of their inner selves. They may be filled with questions, and it's almost like these questions automatically make things more challenging. Even when someone fails to recognize how fortunate they are in a given situation, it doesn't necessarily mean you can benefit from their misfortune. Instead, they may find themselves in the hands of others who are also in search of love and wealth, and they are positioned in the right place where they rightfully belong.

You've found yourself, but true happiness will only come when you fully comprehend your journey. To attain the things you desire in this world, you must earn them by gaining a deep understanding of yourself and your actions. Until you reach a point where you genuinely know and grasp your purpose, you won't achieve anything in this life.

While we aspire to accomplish many goals, there are instances when certain endeavors can become overwhelming due to one's limited comprehension. When a person is confronted with such challenges, relinquishing them may seem like an excessive burden. These are the types of situations where individuals are acutely aware that venturing beyond a certain threshold may leave them vulnerable or susceptible to exploitation.

Many people may wonder why they encounter setbacks in life. It's important to recognize that not everything is meant to go smoothly. Sometimes, when you're not yet at the level you aspire to be, it can feel like everything is working against you. The world can be challenging, but when you have a clear understanding of your identity, many things become easier to handle. What often complicates matters are our own desires and necessities.

Everything we want from life is often a result of our own thoughts and actions. When we don't reach our goals and fall short of the life we desire, it can make us question what went wrong with our well-being.

Sometimes, it's actually beneficial when you face a shortage or a lack of something. This is because it encourages you to explore your own understanding and find solutions. It's important to note that not having all the knowledge expected by society to fit in doesn't mean you can't achieve what you desire in life. While you might feel pressured by the challenges you're going through, remember that everyone has needs in life. Even if you lack certain knowledge, you can still persevere and overcome obstacles.

Sometimes, you may encounter a situation where you have the determination to achieve your goals, but you might not yet possess the means to do so. Frustration can often accompany failure to attain your desired outcomes, especially when you're not quite there yet. However, when your mindset aligns with your aspirations, whether it's through your own insights or by welcoming positivity from the world around you, you'll reap the rewards you truly deserve in this life. Understanding this concept isn't overly complex; it's about embracing the natural course of your creative journey. Even though some individuals may harbor feelings of jealousy, reality cannot truly harm you in your pursuit of success.

A lack of understanding, knowledge, and clarity about certain issues can be quite detrimental. When you don't comprehend why certain events consistently unfold in a particular manner, you can become overwhelmed by confusion. As you progress on your journey and complete the necessary tasks, even without explicit validation, you gain a strong sense of how things should be accomplished, making you indomitable and unstoppable.

Yes, there might not be someone to teach you or help you understand things better, but your mind believes that everything is as it should be. Many people give up when they can't see the results of their efforts at this stage. Instead, try to find real understanding because it leads to lasting success. You shouldn't just take things away from people; they will resist because they value their identity and what's important to them. There is no one who knows everything about our basic needs.

People already have a good understanding of what's happening in that aspect of their lives. Instead of merely imparting knowledge, it's more effective to educate them about the importance of making choices that ensure their safety, rather than finding themselves in a precarious situation. When it comes to the fundamental aspects of life that we all require, it's essential to recognize that extracting those insights from individuals may prove challenging.

Living life this way can be wonderful, but it comes with responsibilities. Many people enter this journey thinking about the uniqueness of achieving something extraordinary, standing out among the crowd. However, we must ask ourselves if we possess the knowledge and skills to navigate this path independently, find love on our own, and secure the necessary finances.

It doesn't matter that money has always had a big impact on doing something. However, sometimes you might lose it. The most important thing we all need for life could suddenly come up. When everyone doesn't want to change who they are, it can really hurt you when someone doesn't give you the love you were expecting. It can be very sad when you can't lift yourself up with your own thoughts and start thinking that the world is against you. You might even try to harm other people's lives.

You were there to teach them about life and relationships, but many of them already know a lot about themselves. Perhaps you can help them learn the importance of valuing one another and treating each other gently. It's not that they don't understand this, but sometimes they forget to appreciate the treasure in each other. You can remind them that missing out on such an opportunity can lead to moments of desperation. When you lose something, it's not easy to recover it quickly.

We often carry a lot with us, and if you ever experience a setback while pursuing something you're knowledgeable about, it can lead to significant consequences. You may find yourself in a place where you once had a deep understanding of life, but now you embody the essence of failure. Everything that defined you is closely tied to what you've lost. This is a valuable lesson to impart to others – the importance of constant vigilance and unwavering dedication to everything they hold dear. It's crucial to realize how much can be at stake if they ever let negligence creep in. Restoring what's been damaged may send them on a quest to rediscover their identity, and the price of such a journey can be quite high.

Our purpose in life is to help people understand the world we inhabit today. Many natural aspects have undergone significant transformations, making it crucial for us to exercise caution. Even though love for one another may come naturally, the constant evolution of human inventions demands our vigilance. We are surrounded by numerous creations that have materialized through human innovation. Thus, we must remain vigilant, keeping an eye out for the ideas that are still eager for realization and are desperate to emerge and fulfill the intentions of their creators.

The inventor's life became a sacrifice to witness the creation of something unknown to people. This is where we all lose something crucial. We lose a part of ourselves when we dedicate so much of our identity and everything we have ever known to a particular vision, forsaking our original selves since we believe in a grand idea.

When you start embracing these thoughts, you gradually start losing the harmony in this life that we've all been granted. It's essential to remember that you shouldn't do things solely to boost your ego; instead, engage in them to re-connect with reality. Don't merely get involved to fit into a particular concept; strive to thrive within its abundance. Aim for a state of equilibrium or dedicate your entire essence to achieving success. Surpass all levels of human dedication, even when it's challenging, and go above and beyond the typical expectations. Challenge yourself to step outside your comfort zone and ultimately reach the place where you aspire to become your true self.

Many people find it hard to let go or break the strong connection they have with life. We tend to cling to elements of our past, even though we should be embracing the future with open arms. Often, we struggle with complete com-mitment, preventing us from truly comprehending the wonder of understand-ing and being fully dedicated. To achieve this, we must give our all, leaving nothing to live for except our dedication. When you stand out in the world, make it clear that you're determined to earn a living through your unique ap-proach, and you won't give up. You'll do whatever it takes to make your dreams a reality.

In contrast to when you used to believe in your past self, a person who aimed for the perfect harmony of all the things that humanity seeks. Back then, you wouldn't find yourself trapped in the repetitiveness of a world where everyone follows the same routine. This is the place where we were meant to lead our lives, but many mysteries remain concealed from us as human beings. This is why it's crucial to welcome diversity and individuality.

Sometimes, we find ourselves yearning to return to that familiar world be-cause we struggle to grasp things with absolute clarity. Failing to fulfill our responsibilities adequately can result in us living a life that falls far short of the expected standards. It's truly disheartening when we make efforts to fit in, but our minds are unable to find equilibrium. We may envision ourselves standing at the crossroads of everyone else's vibrant life, yet we can no longer be an active part of that world. Instead, we are destined to wrestle with our innermost aspirations unless we discover a path to bring them to fruition.

To achieve your vision, it's crucial to be fully dedicated. Don't fear failure, as striving for greatness often demands a lifelong commitment. So, put in your best effort, stay determined, and even if you're unsure about your destination, rely on your inner strength to stay true to yourself and eventually reach your desired destination.

Picture a lifetime where you've never quite found that elusive equilibrium. You've harbored a dream, yet your dedication and discipline haven't been steadfast in its pursuit. It's like you've been unable to steer yourself toward that deserving goal. You've attempted to unlock the door to full-fledged success, but haven't quite made it all the way through, resulting in persistent personal setbacks. Nevertheless, there's no need to sink into the belief that you'll forever be labeled a failure. You possess the ability to uncover the very thing you aspire to become.

If you've decided to dedicate your life to a particular dream or goal, then make an effort to exceed the usual limits of life and delve deeper into your own knowledge. This becomes important when you feel like you can't connect with everyday things or when you're unsure about your path, especially when it seems like the world isn't providing you with much. During these times, your determination can motivate you to reach a place where your aspirations become reality on the other side.

We're not complete failures; the world always gives us opportunities to pursue our dreams and strive for success. With unwavering dedication, you can discover your true self along the way. You'll have the chance to observe your thoughts, identify your aspirations, and leave behind the feeling of being lost. You'll watch your desires turn into reality.

What prevents us from achieving or perhaps surpassing the balance of life? There's so much we didn't grasp about how to do things correctly, how to live in a manner that fulfills that measure of success. It's like a calling; when you respond to the call for prosperity, something stands at the gate to humanity and examines everything about us. If it's content with the dedication we've shown, it grants us what we desire and genuinely deserve from our existence. It's an invitation to embrace the world as it is, and to make a living from it. Alternatively, you can aim to exceed that equilibrium level and reach for the stars.

If you don't achieve your dream, you may never feel content with anything. It can be even more challenging when you fall short of finding that perfect balance in life, and when the world seems to reject everything about you, you may find yourself lost in your own thoughts. As we reach certain points in our lives, there are moments when we can't undo our past choices. How can you recover from such a setback when everything has gone wrong?

Your distinctive perspective on the world can help you attain your desires. It empowers you to correct any mistakes you've made and embrace your true self, navigating life through your own insights. Regardless of your choices, life serves as a valuable teacher. If you fail to learn its lessons, you may find yourself endlessly pursuing something unattainable. Therefore, strive to master your thoughts, pursue your individual path relentlessly, and ultimately achieve success.

As you make your way to the opposite side, you will start to see that everything is as it should be. Can you achieve a sense of balance through your own understanding? Perhaps you can, or maybe not. Nevertheless, endeavor to either attain equilibrium or go beyond it, and embrace your own creative potential. We must acknowledge the gift of humanity to truly be human. To be human, we must accept our roles as citizens who are cared for and who also thrive through our own creations.

You may have faced difficulties along your usual journey, and many things might have been denied to you. But you didn't lose hope because you had faith in something bigger than your failures. Somehow, you held onto the idea of a greater existence, even when you were heading into the unknown. Surprisingly, you managed to make things right in the end, and you no longer see the world as a terrible nightmare. So, how can you genuinely redefine yourself based on your own understanding?

Are you willing to abandon your old self in pursuit of new experiences? How can we release the past and transform our mindset, focusing on achieving success through our own abilities? Is it possible that when you have an idea, you must commit wholeheartedly, giving your all and adapting to circumstances if necessary?

Make a strong commitment to something that nobody can stop you from pursuing. Aim to share your knowledge with the world. Chase after your true self, and remember that love and money won't just fall into your lap – you need to put in the effort to earn them. Don't give up easily. Strive to build a life that you value. If you ever find yourself stuck and unsure of how to move forward, focus on progress. Work towards the future you've envisioned for yourself. When you venture out, discover your unique path, and keep at it until it all starts to make sense.

Chapter Thirteen

No Man's Land

You might stumble upon something that deeply upsets many individuals due to the extraordinary and distinct nature of your idea compared to what most have encountered. Nevertheless, it's essential not to allow fear to dominate your actions. Our identities are shaped not by our choices but by the situations we confront in life. As you approach the conclusion of your journey, it's vital to transform these experiences into your unique reality, determined by your responses to various situations.

No matter how strong your emotions may be, you should never allow anything to hinder your progress toward your goals. Even if you were confident in your actions and carried your aspirations with you, you might not have realized that your actions would clash with existing ideas. As regular human beings, we often focus on how things will unfold from our own point of view and tend to overlook how the rest of the world might react to our actions.

We find ourselves utterly astonished by the emotions we experience, the intricate nature of life, and our unique perspective on the world around us. It's truly something beyond comprehension, this essence of being human. It's as if an enchanting force resides within each of us, enabling us to connect with everything. It becomes an integral part of our existence, and we cannot resist the urge to share this profound sensation with the entire human race.

Once you've spent a lifetime dedicated to expanding your knowledge and exploring the boundaries of understanding, you may come across individuals who share similar interests and passions. As you engage with these like-minded individuals, you might discover that your opinions and perspectives sometimes clash due to your differing viewpoints. In these moments, you may reflect and wonder how you let these contrasting perspectives influence your own viewpoint, ultimately shaping your perspective and influencing your decision-making process.

Why did I get involved in something like this? You might feel scared because you've let certain thoughts influence your belief in your ability to succeed. As a young person in this complex world, relying on your own knowledge can lead to uncertainty. Not being sure if everything will work out and if you're heading in the right direction can be worrisome. On the flip side, fear can infiltrate every aspect of your whole self, to the point where you might consider altering your original intentions.

You can't always predict the direction your path will take, and sometimes, you might stumble upon an idea without realizing it'll eventually replace another or become a vital part of something bigger. Later on, you might discover that similar concepts existed before yours, but perhaps they didn't succeed because they lacked the dedication needed to provide the quality care society demands.

When individuals experience dissatisfaction with their lives, they often feel compelled to explore alternative paths or create new solutions that can enhance their well-being. If you, as someone who is curious about improving your overall quality of life, find yourself developing novel ideas for improvement, these ideas may sometimes clash with established concepts. Depending on the depth of your understanding, you may ponder whether there is cause for concern about persisting in your pursuit of the right course of action in the face of significant opposition.

If you truly mean well, you should know that the world is for everyone who lives in it. Even if you've been doing things right, if the world needs your help, you should step up. Perhaps it's time for the universe to see things from your point of view, and you should accept that idea. What would you like to accomplish in the future? Sometimes, you might feel lost in the beginning, but eventually, you'll find your way and gain a better understanding of what you're meant to do and how valuable your talents are.

You start to understand that your gift is incredibly significant, and it should never be underestimated, not even in comparison to anything that has come before or could have existed in the past. You also deserve a second opportunity. You might have faced failures in your endeavors, only to uncover your true purpose along a unique journey that grants your life a profound sense of purpose. Strangely enough, the talent you've unearthed within yourself can hold immense importance for the person you are, as it can help many things become clearer by aiding people in comprehending it.

If you were to abandon this idea, what would occupy the remaining years of your life? Could you face the possibility of harboring profound regrets for forsaking the sole potentiality that might have bestowed purpose upon your entire existence? The vast expanse of knowledge and experiences in our world remains largely uncharted until you embark on your personal odyssey. Consequently, we are consistently invigorated by the prospect of creation before we can gain comprehensive insight into it. Your thoughts and actions wield considerable influence; the more deeply you immerse yourself in an endeavor, the greater the likelihood of uncovering profound insights about it and discovering ways to enhance the well-being of humanity through your contributions.

You should recognize that it's entirely possible for you to be continuously astonished by the incredible achievements of others and to think to yourself, "Wow, what an astonishing world full of marvels!" Nevertheless, it's important to understand that you possess similar abilities deep within yourself. The only difference is that you might need to make certain sacrifices to embrace the transformation on this new journey you've embarked upon.

If you fully dedicate yourself to a truly sincere pursuit with all your heart, you might find yourself pleasantly astonished by the astonishing marvels of the world. You could even surpass those individuals you once believed had achieved remarkable feats in their lives. It's important to note that the essence of creation doesn't diminish their significance; in fact, it magnifies it. By exploring a nascent universe in its early stages, they have forged a unique perspective that has, in turn, illuminated the path for numerous others to comprehend the profound impact of their knowledge and actions.

Sometimes, it might take a really long time for you to realize something wonderful about yourself that you never knew existed. You may not have understood your own abilities or significance until that moment. Perhaps, for a while, you thought you weren't capable of achieving anything remarkable. Then one day, you uncovered a hidden talent within you, and suddenly, everything changed. You might have thought the world could function just fine without this talent, but in truth, it's an essential piece of the puzzle. Sometimes, you need to realize that this journey may have only just begun, and it requires every aspect of who you are to make sense of the universe.

You might have experienced deep shame about your past self, long before you achieved something significant in your life. You might have seen yourself as embarrassing in everything you attempted, and nothing seemed to make sense. Every time you tried something, it felt like a source of shame, making you doubt your competence and self-worth. You may have harbored anger towards the world you lived in, feeling like the only person unsure about how others navigate through life's challenges.

Deep within your inner self, you might ponder about your journey, contemplating how a special talent could uncover itself in the midst of obscurity. Perhaps, you weren't fully prepared for the complexities of the world, dedicating yourself diligently, only to find that the timing wasn't right for all the pieces to align perfectly. In your thoughts, you understood that you were inherently ordinary, but the world around you failed to acknowledge your uniqueness, particularly because it wasn't something you could easily reveal to others. Instead, you had to guard it closely within your heart.

Things can seem amusing if you're not accustomed to the world we inhabit. You might experience a sense of being adrift, for the world has its established routines, and people are generally considered regular if they conform to these routines. This becomes particularly evident when you're grappling with the pursuit of an elusive goal. This pursuit can transform you in ways you never comprehended, especially when you endeavor to bring your aspirations to life by relying on your own comprehension.

You found yourself in the world of creativity, where you lived your life just like everyone else. You worked every day to improve your understanding, and slowly, things started to make sense. At first, you didn't really know who you were. However, as you continued to do things your way, you began to see the light, especially in places where you had previously felt lost. Fitting in with everyone else was challenging because you didn't experience creativity the same way they did. Your unique way of processing information was through your own efforts, and that's what made you feel normal.

As intelligent human beings, we have a unique ability to comprehend and engage with things that others might not have explored yet. This capability empowers us to embark on a journey towards a more promising future. It involves not only identifying this path but also cultivating self-discipline along this newfound route. Without a profound purpose driving us from within, our existence might seem devoid of significance to the broader world.

This is how life can lead you on a journey to find yourself. You become disciplined in the talent or path you've chosen for yourself. We are ordinary people who sense the world around us after uncovering our purpose: to love everything that exists. Indeed, the external world differs from the universe we've found within ourselves. Your personal discovery requires you to fully comprehend whatever you're doing to find contentment. It's a way for you to recognize your true potential.

This type of comprehension plays a crucial role in influencing the everyday world we encounter. However, the actuality inside may often clash with the vast external world. When you find yourself unfamiliar with the cosmos, lacking knowledge about the intricacies of creation, you must rely solely on your creativity and dedication to transform into an ordinary individual.

Life can be quite puzzling when it lacks clarity, but when you start grasping the mysteries of existence, it becomes challenging to revert to the old ways of life. You grow more confident, composed, and resolute in your pursuit of success because you've acquired the knowledge of how things should be done. After enduring a path that never provided what defines you, how can you simply forsake your identity or subject yourself to disappointment once more?

The world might be different from what you've known before. When the moment arrived for you to return to a regular routine, you felt an urge to become someone of significance through that journey, as you might have previously lacked common sense in many aspects of your comprehension. Nonetheless, at present, everything holds the significance it should, because you've discovered something immensely important to live for, and you are dedicated to it.

For the very first time, you are experiencing a profound sense of happiness because you've discovered a specific purpose to live for. Nevertheless, there are moments when your past resurfaces, causing disruptions and haunting thoughts that hinder your forward journey. Nonetheless, currently, you are on a path to healing and rejuvenation, and your life has commenced to acquire meaning in all your endeavors. The phase where you struggled to comprehend your true self did not endure indefinitely. As you embarked upon the threshold of a significant breakthrough, before you even realized it, you became fully prepared to live your entire existence with absolute clarity regarding your life's purpose and what you strive for.

Building your own world can be a challenging endeavor. Along the way, you may encounter various obstacles and difficulties. However, if you persist with a kind and positive mindset, you will ultimately discover your rightful place. Many obstacles may obstruct a person's path to their destiny, but you will overcome whatever problems lie before you. These challenges may not have been part of your original plan, but they could be the key to rediscovering your sense of significance as a regular, purpose-driven human being committed to achieving success.

Living in your own world, where you create your own path and understand everything that comes your way, can sometimes seem impossible. It can be quite challenging, drawing upon your knowledge, but you manage to overcome all obstacles on your journey to making your thoughts a reality. It takes patience for things to happen, yet you carry the bright light of intelligence with confidence, believing in a brighter future that lies ahead.

In the past, things were different. You might have noticed that some people judge your way of life because you haven't yet found complete satisfaction in the journey you've embarked on. These individuals appear to be at ease with their own beliefs, having come to a deeper understanding of their true selves and finding purpose in their desires.

You might have once found yourself not knowing much about how people live their lives. This happens frequently, and you often felt confused, especially when everyone around you was going about their human routines, which seemed quite puzzling to you. It was a bit disheartening because many appeared to be having a great time with everything going on in their chosen paths. It bothered you deep down to witness people living in a way that was unfamiliar to you, especially when it came to their daily survival.

In the world where you wandered away from your chosen path, you might not feel good about yourself. You might always be asking yourself how you ended up lost, and you may continually underestimate the fact that you didn't find a clear path to follow. However, if, despite everything that has happened, you manage to discover a way to become the person you want to be, you will feel a sense of validation. You'll realize that you weren't aimlessly wandering;

there was a purpose calling you to this life, and there is so much to live for. While you may not have been content with the life you were living when you looked at it from the outside, deep down, you were always aware of your true self and what you were capable of. It's just that you couldn't find the connection to your inner being.

It's a wonderful feeling to realize that after a considerable period of uncertainty, you eventually found a purposeful path to follow in life. During your journey, you might have encountered individuals who are self-centered and overly forceful in pursuing their desires, which can be unsettling when you're striving to establish your own significance. While it's true that there were many moments when you didn't grasp everything completely, it's essential to remember that nobody should impose their desires on you.

As you continue to mature, you will gradually realize that at each stage of life, there is something valuable to appreciate. However, sometimes, others might refuse to grant you the opportunity to be a part of those experiences. Perhaps you might have encountered obstacles that hindered your determination to achieve your goals. Yet, when you are the creator of your own path, you bring your entire self to navigate even in the absence of a clear route.

We are not inherently aware that the world can be a harsh and unforgiving place, where many of our dreams may not materialize as we envisioned. However, our personal aspirations help us comprehend the inner workings of everything.

Just imagine being a person living their one and only life, which you've become really good at. You don't need to pause or question what you're doing, or contemplate returning to your old self when you face difficulties, as this might make you lose your true self forever. You pour your entire heart into your efforts, even when you can't figure out the path forward, but you have faith in the core idea that has shaped your outlook, and you stay committed until everything you're familiar with brings your dreams to life.

Even though your ideas may vary greatly from others, you should not become anxious. You see, the realm of creativity doesn't exclusively pertain to any single person; rather, it is open to all individuals, both men and women, who wholeheartedly commit themselves to pursuing excellence. Their names shall be etched into this creative realm, and your name shall find its place among them, right there, in the very heart of where life takes form.

You might miss out on a chance to lead a regular life if you let other ideas that exist in the world intimidate you. Remember, you have a place too, and your contributions are part of what has shaped the world as we know it today. While it's natural to aspire to make a difference in areas that others have explored before, genuine creativity seeks to delve deeper into realms of knowledge where fewer have ventured before.

Creativity often encounters gaps, and individuals frequently find themselves driven to make meaningful contributions to their lives. The universe continually seeks input to enhance the human experience, and you may well be the individual required to fill that void with your valuable knowledge and talents.

As the world progresses, there is often a void that must be filled, which emerges when individuals struggle to fully comprehend themselves or various matters. This gap is not easily sealed, for nothing is ever truly whole, yet it presents a remarkable opportunity for numerous individuals to embark on a journey of self-discovery. It is our destiny to uncover our true selves through the exploration of the world around us. Even when people believe they have accomplished everything, there remains a potential for them to contribute to the improvement of human life.

We have many tasks ahead of us as we seek to rediscover our true selves in the places where we may have lost sight of them. Both love and happiness rely on this journey. During the times when you were unsure of your whereabouts, various circumstances may have attempted to challenge you. Now is the opportune moment to address and correct some of the mistakes you may have made during that period.

Choosing a unique path in life doesn't mean you're devoid of true love; you indeed possess it. It's possible that, at times, you might have been held back due to your unwavering commitment to your work and the goals you've dedicated yourself to achieving.

When you find yourself facing challenging circumstances, love can sometimes be influenced to act against your interests. Relationships play a significant role in our lives and often have a substantial impact on our prospects for success. When someone is in a stable relationship, it can serve as a crucial factor in unlocking your inner happiness. This is because every aspect of life comes with its own set of responsibilities, and these responsibilities have now become a necessity.

When you've been searching for yourself for a long time, you might end up feeling like no one cares about you, especially when you go through the changes that are bound to happen. If you don't fully understand things, they often don't go the way you want them to, and this is normal because you might be at the beginning of your life journey. But when it comes to the idea of love in the grand scheme of creation, it shouldn't be viewed as a problem. Remember, you're not alone on this journey, and anything you do that you're unsure about can sometimes make things more challenging for everyone involved.

No matter how things may have appeared to you, when you work, remember that you will discover something extraordinary in the end. Your growth will enable you to deeply connect with someone truly valuable to us as human beings. You might have to let certain individuals go because the type of relationship you desire might have distinct prerequisites for someone who has gained wisdom through their personal experiences. There are characteristics that, as a human being, you might seek in a person, and these qualities could be challenging to come across given the many transformations in the world.

Although you could have started alone, you might come across someone who can provide you with strength through their genuine love and support at every stage of your life. When you meet such a person, concentrate on demonstrating your love, compassion, and the significance they hold in your personal growth. A valuable relationship is one where someone truly cares about you, respects your choices, and stands by you from the moment you unite. They become a dependable presence, unwavering in their commitment to each other, ensuring care for the remainder of your lives.

The individual you choose to welcome into your life should bring blessings that make you both value each other's company and delve deeper into each other's lives. Within your heart, you should strive to bring blessings to one another that help you forget the challenges you've faced.

You might find yourself alone at times. Nevertheless, wholehearted dedication to putting in effort will unlock something within you. It will help you discover your purpose in every endeavor you undertake. Even if you've faced strong dislike to the point where people couldn't bear to be around you, when the moment arrives and you've fulfilled your responsibilities, you'll be capable of attracting the enduring love you've always sought.

As you overcome each challenge on your journey, you'll witness things you once considered incredibly tough becoming a reality, perhaps even enduring beyond your expectations. At some point in our lives, regardless of our origins, we dedicate ourselves to witnessing the seemingly impossible come to fruition in our world. This commitment can break any chains that may have restrained you from abundance.

Throughout your entire life, you may have experienced discrimination, but if you harbor something truly remarkable within yourself, it will inevitably emerge. This inner greatness will guide you, eliminating any uncertainty about your identity and your knowledge. Our world has a rich history, and to achieve success, it is essential to have unwavering faith in your ability to carve a path, even in the face of seemingly insurmountable obstacles.

True value is something that you can only attain when you put in a lot of effort to build up your understanding. It's about cherishing your unique way of thinking and letting your thoughts shape your inner desires. When you have this kind of determination, you start to make your deepest wishes come true. It doesn't matter where you come from; you might belong to a place where people have never been recognized for who they are. However, you could break that pattern and become the trailblazer who changes everything.

To truly commit, you must believe in yourself and your worthiness to be the best. Consider if it brings greater satisfaction to be second best or simply follow in someone's path. Perhaps, you might find contentment by sitting beside them?

Imagine if you were the very first person to desire something with an intensity that surpassed what most people could even dream of. You yearn to gain recognition for this unique aspiration. You carry a burning desire to be acknowledged for the unwavering dedication you've poured into this endeavor. You firmly believe that you should have the chance to be honored, given that you've devoted your entire existence to witnessing the transformation of your dreams into attainable realities.

Do you think anyone can stop you if you truly grasp what you're doing and have completed all the necessary steps to excel? You might never comprehend what shaped another person, but genuine dedication to our heartfelt endeavors can unearth hidden aspects of yourself. Have you attempted to connect with your inner self and explored every corner of your being? These queries may persist within your spirit, yet diligent effort can unveil the precise answers you sought at the outset of your expedition.

We often believe we've done what we can, but our efforts may not always be recognized. However, when you fully accomplish your goals and go above and beyond to excel, your efforts will eventually yield results. Explore all possibilities without fear or doubt, and in the end, you may unlock opportunities that others, including those from your own circle, have not. You can confidently stride towards your destiny without any hindrances.

If you truly have confidence in your actions, you have the potential to become a highly significant individual. Your influence could extend far and wide, and your presence may leave an indelible mark. However, this will only transpire if you wholeheartedly commit yourself to achieving a specific goal. This dedication will bring you into the spotlight effortlessly; you won't even need to struggle for it. It will be a destined path for you to traverse. Once it aligns with your true purpose, you cannot evade it; it is an essential part of being human. Failing to pursue this particular calling raises questions about your inner self. To live authentically, you must exert effort, understand your identity, and find your rightful place.

When you've put your absolute best effort into pursuing your deepest desires, your path will become forever clear. The love you hold for both the world and that special person will discover the perfect place to reside. You hail from a unique background, and as you gaze upon creation, even though your talents may be present, circumstances don't always align with your prior expectations. It may appear rather daunting, and we're often not completely prepared for it. It's unfortunate how one can become ensnared by various distractions, to the point where even the communities of our upbringing lose significance, as your focus has always been the vast universe, shaped by your profound comprehension.

Our longing for the world resembled this: we were facing a life that wouldn't be easy to attain. Some might find solace in the idea that when certain goals seem impossible to achieve, there will always be another opportunity waiting to be seized. These challenging situations can be perplexing, but I want to emphasize that the door you must enter will remain open indefinitely, and it will always be your choice to take action. However, some people don't have the refuge of an escape when their efforts fall short. For them, the path forward is to remain steadfastly dedicated to their global aspirations.

There are many things we must achieve in order to find complete happiness. Two essential components for contentment are money and love, which cannot be underestimated. However, numerous obstacles may hinder our progress to the point where it feels impossible. Keeping our goals in mind does not necessarily simplify our journey; in fact, it may require us to confront the complexities of the world. When you pursue something you've created for yourself, devote your attention to doing your very best to increase your chances of success. Often, there are numerous challenges between a person and their destiny, leaving us to wonder how some individuals overcome them. Perhaps the solution lies in hard work and the patience to fully comprehend every aspect of the journey.

The world, as we understand it, may not appear as bleak as some might suggest. Nevertheless, being closely tied to our comprehension can pose considerable challenges. Many aspects that were once familiar can vanish from our knowledge. Life might have been simpler in various ways. Nevertheless, the goals we aim to accomplish in our individual circumstances can make life arduous. This is due to the formalities inherent in the act of creation.

Can your relentless dedication truly validate your aspirations? There must be a source of solace that fills your heart, especially when you've poured every ounce of your being into your endeavors, including the tiniest reservoirs of inner strength. When the formidable challenges of the world confront you, and you turn inward to assess your intrinsic value, that's when you summon your reservoir of knowledge and resilience. You transform into the very embodiment of your desires, becoming precisely what you sought from the vast universe.

As you ponder, you come to understand that at our core, we all share a common drive and enthusiasm for life, albeit expressed uniquely. What propels someone to take action is precisely what inspires another to pursue their desires. We aspire to similar outcomes in all aspects of existence, yet the distinction lies in how each individual chooses to utilize their drive and what path they forge with their aspirations.

There are no exceptions to this rule. What we require is shown by the dedication one must give. However, when you reflect on yourself, you might sense that you have gone above and beyond what is typically acceptable. Therefore, if you genuinely want to achieve your desires, you may need to put in extra effort beyond the usual standards. This is because you might not be aware of the efforts others have put in to reach their current positions.

You can't predict everything life holds, but if you truly commit to your goals and work with determination, you'll find that many things can alter your circumstances. When you stay dedicated, unnecessary elements will fade away, leaving room for something better. What fades away within you will clear a path for what you long for, and as you continue on that path, you'll move towards a brighter future. When you truly understand what you're doing, your desires will consistently shape your journey towards achieving everything you need.

You won't be stuck in one place forever as you work towards your destination. Eventually, something will come along to help you reach your intended goal. If you've discovered what truly drives you, you'll naturally find your place in the world. Everything you know and possess has a place in this world, even if you haven't figured out how it fits into human life at this moment.

Knowledge serves a crucial purpose by offering closure and comprehension. It helps individuals become more conscious of the life they are experiencing, thereby providing direction for their efforts. With this heightened awareness and dedication to their pursuits, one can unlock the fullest potential of their existence. On the contrary, remaining unaware of one's circumstances can obscure the hidden capabilities present within every human being, leading to unrealized opportunities.

Chapter Fourteen

Concrete Foundation

You're embarking on a journey to discover your true self. Are you confident about the steps to take in order to make a remarkable entrance into the world? How do you plan not just to gain recognition for something but to be among the very best, becoming one of the most significant individuals that the world has ever known? So, the question arises: Do you possess the qualities and qualities that have shaped your perspective deep within, or are you merely seeking a lasting place in the thoughts of everyone you encounter? Which aspect of your being will leave a lasting impression in the minds of those you interact with?

This is where we're likely to establish our ideas. Everything we say flows through this path, which reveals the type of person you are. It shapes our character, defining the person who engages with humanity. You're perceived through the values instilled in you since the start of your life. It doesn't just inform others about you; it propels you from your very core, gaining strength as it seeks its place in people's lives. As a living concept, it discovers its rightful spot in the world.

Not everyone has the ability to create such a character. Especially one that will become an integral part of people's lives and not just shows sympathy for humanity but also comprehends the daily struggles of human beings. This kind of discipline needs constant practice until it becomes an inherent part of your personality. We are not naturally born with this level of understanding, but it's a quality we develop through awareness and how we react to the world around us.

People possess diverse viewpoints that shape their identities, primarily influenced by their unique perspectives. Nevertheless, there exists something akin to an intrinsic essence that defines our significance in this world, surpassing mere aspirations for a specific lifestyle. Indeed, some individuals ground their self-conceptions in certain desires and permit these desires to govern their decision-making processes. These lives are not anchored in guiding principles but are steered by the pursuit of particular objectives.

You have the opportunity to let your thoughts influence your understanding. This can provide you with a chance to obtain something you deeply desire, which could be something very important to you. Consequently, this can play a role in shaping the way you perceive and experience reality in your daily life.

When you let a specific need you have for a brand or something special affect who you are, you might not reach the depths of your inner self, where the fundamental principles reside. It's important to ponder what truly defines success in both the short term and the long run. Is it the way we communicate our thoughts and ideas? Keep in mind that the way you think from this standpoint is how others will perceive you, and this perception can lead to either affection or aversion based on your understanding. But can it genuinely shape the course of our lives?

Many times, we find ourselves pondering the reasons behind our thoughts, often unaware of the influences shaping our beliefs. It can be challenging to discern whether our convictions stem from sincere origins, and it's easy to miss the profound essence within us where our true selves reside, thinking independently. If you aspire to connect with people on a deeper level, you might contemplate the intricacies of human existence and the manner in which we navigate life. As an individual, your desire to be recognized for something genuine and meaningful should outweigh any inclination to merely seize opportunities for personal gain.

It's clear that the way we go about our daily lives, from the meals we consume to the garments we put on and the vehicles we utilize, is shaped by particular brands or ideologies established by individuals. We strive towards these ideals with great dedication. If you don't delve deep into your own beliefs, you might not fully comprehend your identity or the principles you uphold. In fact, those principles might not even exist. Many of us are driven by the pursuit of specific goals, which is a fundamental aspect of human existence.

If we can ever attain a profound understanding and a solid foundation for life, it profoundly shapes our reality. This, in turn, influences how we approach the world, and it lays the groundwork for developing our ideas. Therefore, it is crucial to grasp the significance of pushing oneself to delve deeper until reaching a point where the motivation goes beyond mere luxury. It becomes an opportunity to convey a meaningful message that can contribute to enhancing human lives. Reaching this point enables one to connect with the broader spectrum of humanity, as it represents a shared aspect of our human experience.

What if you haven't quite reached the core of understanding? Is it okay to let the world around us shape our thoughts? Even if our preferences differ, can we still form meaningful connections and reach common ground as human beings, no matter how strongly we hold onto our personal likes and dislikes?

While we often overlook the connections we share with everything in our surroundings, it's essential to recognize that if you haven't reached the core from which you can build your identity, then you are left with very little. You can either draw inspiration from your inner self or the external world, as one of these should guide you in understanding the broader global context. If you haven't delved deep within to grasp the profound truth seeking expression through you, then all you can do is interpret the things you encounter in your daily life.

No matter how you view the world, you may discover a role within people's lives. This is because we all strive for greatness and yearn to achieve something significant. This desire forms the basis for our connections with others as we join forces to make our dreams come true. Even if you sometimes struggle to connect with your inner self, you might benefit from establishing a robust bond with a well-established brand. Without this connection, your public image may suffer, and you may not rank among the top choices available.

What determines the types of ideas we hold? Deep within our thoughts, we are still human, and a part of us thinks like every other person. Commitment plays a crucial role in how we dedicate ourselves to an idea, and when we commit fully to one, we may find ourselves without any other roles to play as humans. This can help us maintain focus and avoid drifting in different directions. When we are wholly dedicated to a particular way of life, we develop a heightened awareness. Our voice is then meant to express or write about what we observe, and everything around us affects us as we are part of the creative process. If we choose silence, we risk losing ourselves entirely.

Should we focus on establishing our foundation before tackling other aspects of life? As humans, we can't ignore the world around us and how it shapes us. We should explore the vastness of existence and put in the effort to help people understand themselves better. We shouldn't shy away from deep understanding and awareness. Instead, we should strive to create meaning from the entirety of life.

We start by setting our guiding principles to create a solid foundation. This helps us define what we stand for in a way that people can easily grasp. It also ensures that we remain steadfast in our beliefs, resisting attempts to alter our perspective on the broader picture. While you may not yet have a clear picture of the world that lies ahead, you have carefully contemplated the things that give your life purpose and hold them dear. As you continue to grow, you strive to discover a space where your ideas find their rightful home.

We don't fully understand the origins of the world we inhabit today, but we find comfort in the belief that a better world exists, designed to accommodate humanity effortlessly. Therefore, when embarking on this journey of life, let us refrain from actions that undermine the very essence of creation. Instead, let us commit ourselves to the noble pursuit of fostering positivity in our sur-roundings. Consider how, in the past, you may have yearned for treatment akin to what you now provide: acknowledgement that your existence holds significance in relation to others. Strive to avoid being perceived as adrift, and aim to touch the depths of others' hearts with your actions.

We should choose ideas that can lead us to a broader path. This path will guide us to the kind of life we want to live. As we journey along this path, we should be aware that no matter what challenges we face, we are heading to-wards a place where everything we do is warmly embraced and accepted.

In order to achieve success, it's important that our thoughts are in harmony with bigger ideas, which might be somewhat similar, yet significantly robust, almost like a comforting home where everything that makes you who you are can find a peaceful place to settle. This consistent alignment is like a reassuring guide in our lives, reassuring us that if we've made the right choices, we will ultimately reach our rightful destination. Therefore, it's crucial not to engage in activities that are unrelated to the core values and aspirations of the people around us, as this could lead to a lack of reception or understanding. Even though we are young and inexperienced, we can be compared to infants who need nourishment to grow and make a meaningful impact on the world we live in.

Don't be shocked if you keep struggling to find where you fit in. It might suggest that what you are hasn't yet met all the requirements. Every concept has a source, and every individual has a place. You must put in consistent effort and never give up until you reach your destined spot. Then, you'll discover that what you are is a part of a bigger idea.

When we are truthful and sincere, everything that defines us is symbolized by a specific world. This world is tangible and accurately corresponds to our true selves. Even if you don't always find it entertaining, somehow, it mirrors your identity and serves as your sanctuary. You may choose to deny it, but you are an integral part of the collective that embodies your essence on a broader scale, and you share a profound connection with those you motivate. Collectively, you shape a vast community with an intricate hierarchy, becoming a bridge to life itself, linking the world you perceive with the global community.

You should grasp the fact that in various corners of the world, there exist individuals who lack the ability to perceive their surroundings fully, and there are concepts that elude the comprehension of many. Your role lies in enlightening them with your insight, allowing them to gain awareness of current events. Instead of remaining in ignorance, they can then exhibit concern or a heightened level of interest. Your place of origin bears no significance; rather, if you possess a radiant persona, you may find it necessary to illuminate the path. Consider the profound impact you could make by facilitating the comprehension of fellow human beings or by prompting them to recognize ways in which they can assist those who are in dire need.

Your duty is to ensure that you generate an idea that won't be viewed as out of place. You must stand as a representative of something you genuinely believe is a significant concern in people's lives. Make it something that captures everyone's attention and becomes a substantial contributor to human well-being. You should also aim to reflect a deep understanding and solid knowledge of the subject matter.

Even when many people don't comprehend, within yourself, you possess the certainty that you are right. You remain unwavering because you've fulfilled your responsibilities with diligence. So, no matter your aspirations, you are not entirely isolated; there exists a broader reality that extends beyond your thoughts. This reality stands ready to embrace and aid in the realization of all your desires.

You should never embark on a solitary quest in search of the nonexistent or merely to secure sufficient support to create a place you can rightfully call your abode, where you are wholeheartedly embraced. There exists a broader world that adheres to the same principles as your own, albeit yours being the lesser of the two, and it is designed to aid you in attaining your objectives. In some way, it exists with the purpose of affording you a foundation upon which you can confidently take a stand and freely articulate your comprehension.

Putting in a lot of effort to achieve your goals will guide you to a place where your ideas can grow and be shared with the world. It might be difficult to believe, but you'll also be able to offer that same kind of love and acceptance to those who seek it from you.

We aren't just individuals who trust our own thoughts and ideas. Instead, we rely on one another to grow as individuals, expand our horizons, and become something greater. Our purpose is to support each other in thriving, as it's crucial to have confidence that in the world where you're meant to be, you hold significant importance. Your presence is essential to the current state of existence. It's vital to grasp that if you don't contribute value to what's already present, you let down those who believe in you. Your worth is substantial, and you belong to a level where your impact is visible in people's lives.

If you ever find yourself in search of genuine happiness and a sense of purpose, then cling steadfastly to your desires, no matter how overwhelming your feelings of despair may become. Always bear in mind that there are individuals out there who share your aspirations. Therefore, if you have invested ample effort into comprehensively grasping every facet of your endeavors, you are capable of making a meaningful contribution to the collective endeavor.

Put in a lot of effort, aim to excel in whatever you're passionate about. Be confident that there's a bigger reality that believes in you, like a reflection of your hard work. Strive for greatness, knowing that the dedication you show to your ideas will also be present when you seek your true self. Avoid encountering an inadequate version of yourself that lacks the qualities to make you stand out; you wouldn't want that for yourself either.

No matter how unique you may seem, someone out there genuinely appreciates the dedication you carry within you. Sometimes, while striving to reach your desired level, you may feel confined, but it can be quite gratifying to know that something extraordinary awaits in the real world. This means you're not wasting your time because you're truly committed. You may not have fully realized why this level of dedication is necessary, but we all understand that the world only reserves a place for greatness. If you don't belong there, then there might be no need to do it all. We act like magnets, attracting precisely what we are destined for, and if you ever stumble, the chances of altering that destiny are ever so slight.

Take a moment to see how reassuring it can be when you truly desire something and have a strong chance of achieving it, even if we have different perspectives on the world. There's a force out there that cares about who we are as individuals. Now, the challenge lies in pursuing your desires while understanding that they aren't a replacement for your true purpose but rather a yearning for greatness. It's essential to grasp that at some point in life, we all need to fully commit to what we require, as our well-being depends on it. This commitment serves as the path to fulfillment; otherwise, we won't truly live.

This might be the type of situation where you need to make a decision at this very moment. What you're striving for in life is what we should consider. The key to success is simply working diligently on a specific goal. If this goal is something that many people pursue in their lives, could it motivate you to put in a bit more effort than you currently are? Try looking at the world from this point of view.

This concept we must embrace and have trust in is similar to the deity we worship. It should possess the capability to respond to all of our requests and bring forth our most profound desires. However, it's important to understand that you won't be able to witness the remarkable wonders of life unless you maintain unwavering faith in this concept. Your steadfast belief in it has the power to transform it into a tangible reality.

If something makes sense, it means it's showing a particular way that has shaped your understanding. When it's relevant and true, you'll discover a spot where you're valued. This concept, which is the bigger picture of the idea you stand for, strives to turn your dreams into actuality. It's here to link you with the real world. It doesn't necessarily have to align exactly with your commitment; it could be about shared values. That's where we find common ground, and that's sufficient.

Have strong faith in yourself. Dedicate your whole self to making something happen. When you get there, it will define who you are because you've devoted your life to it. If you're clear about your principles, nothing can stop you from achieving your purpose. There are many resources available to support you in realizing your dreams as we navigate the world around us.

If you manage to reach that point, you've fulfilled your role because it's crucial to grasp that the world never stops producing things to help you. When you step onto that platform with your comprehension, you effortlessly discover your spot. The act of creation is an ongoing process. Nevertheless, if you haven't pushed yourself to attain that level, you may not fully recognize your potential. You'll only understand that you may need to be firmly rooted in a well-defined idea to make a meaningful impact.

If you really want to explore the vast world and be someone extraordinary, someone who looks out for your safety and well-being, then you should have an idea that connects to this grander vision. In this vast world, you need to discover something that sets you apart, something unique and special about everything you undertake. You wouldn't want to struggle with a common idea; instead, strive to stand out from the crowd, infusing a touch of creativity that captivates everyone's attention. Once you've done your part, the world will come to your aid and propel you toward success, having fulfilled everything necessary to attain a deeper understanding and freedom.

Starting with a simple notion, we embark on our journey. As life progresses, embracing unwavering determination becomes crucial, allowing the enchantment of creativity to flourish within you. When facing obstacles as daunting as mountains, don't offer only a fraction of yourself; give your entirety, leaving nothing behind. Do not withhold even a trace of your energy. Channel it into endeavors that shape your entire being. Approach these tasks with precision and unwavering commitment.

Never hesitate to put in the effort and work diligently. Aim to overcome challenges and demonstrate to yourself that your chosen way of living is sensible. Have confidence that what you say is meaningful. Trust that success is the result of pursuing meaningful ideas, and don't hesitate to pursue them because you know you have a place in the world. It's only when your actions lack purpose that your efforts become futile, and it's during those times that you might struggle to find your place because there's no room for incompetence in creating something meaningful.

You might find yourself as a young individual entangled in a world that has deprived you of everything, leaving you with nothing to display. If this truly carries significant importance to you, you may discover that you've lost your understanding of yourself, and it's truly disheartening to see how you've become disconnected from this realm of thoughts and ideas.

You should recognize that you weren't left alone. You didn't see or fully grasp your actions. If you can release all notions that go beyond becoming the best version of yourself, you'll experience a more profound reality collaborating with you to bring your aspirations to life. Even if the idea you hold isn't the absolute best among all possibilities, understand that it has its own niche. Just make sure not to lose your dedication and stay inspired to play your role, because it's a fact that not everyone can be the very top.

If you don't want to be on a team with people who always lose, you should try your best to come up with a winning idea. Create something powerful and genuine that can make a real difference. Make sure you do your part accurately and well. If you do all this, you'll be on the right path.

Once your beliefs are firmly rooted in what you want to achieve, there's no turning back. You need to show others what you're capable of. Even though we may not all have a lot of knowledge, if you have a strong commitment, you can do extraordinary things.

The key to achieving greatness might be knowing exactly what you want to do for the rest of your life.

Prepare yourself to bring something truly remarkable into existence, especially on the grand scale of greatness that you aspire to be a part of. Think of us as interconnected, like the individual strings of a piano, each producing a distinct note. However, without the presence of the others, you'd never create a harmonious melody. Regardless of your perception of yourself or others, can you recognize the extent to which we rely on one another and the world around us? It's been quite a lengthy journey, and it's unfortunate that you've chosen to become the person you are without knowing what lies ahead. Regrettably, you cannot revert to your former self now that it's too late.

Sometimes, we might think we can change who we are when we face challenges. However, to achieve success, you need to commit fully, leaving behind the past. The only choice should be to move forward. If you still have thoughts about being something else in the past, your idea isn't well-defined. While it can be difficult to fully understand things, you must expand your perspective. This way, as the past fades away, you can set your sights on a larger world ahead.

You can start by thinking of something as a small idea, but don't underestimate its potential. It has the power to evolve into a magnificent creation, even a vast world of its own. Your understanding might be the missing piece in the entire universe. So, as you venture forward, don't confine yourself to a specific area. You have the potential to achieve greatness and establish a way of life that ranks among the best ever created. The key is to immerse yourself so deeply in creativity that there's no turning back. In doing so, a new reality unfolds, shaping your daily existence.

Once you make a deep commitment with your whole heart, it becomes ingrained in your very being, and there's no turning back. This means that you can't simply forget about it or change who you are. Instead of just gazing at a small world, you might consider that this doesn't really bring healing to your inner self. However, if you're enthusiastic about exploring the extent of your capabilities and connecting with everything that exists, you can accomplish remarkable feats with the knowledge you possess. Strive to become more deeply engaged with every idea that shares your passion, nurturing a fervor for greatness. Remember that we don't rely solely on one idea; we are interconnected with many, and your purpose is not to create divisions among them.

Be willing to explore all the options around you. We've managed to handle a lot that's out there. Perhaps our main task is to do our jobs as well as we can and aim for perfection. You never really know what might happen to fulfill your desires. Think about being the weakest link in a team. This is where you should try to contribute something competitive and make a difference when needed. You might not have always had a natural talent for understanding things the way they are, but your goals can justify who you are. You just need to persevere and put in a lot of effort to make them come true.

Your desires play a crucial role in your journey. When you align your energy with your desires, you'll begin to discover many things unfolding along the way, ultimately leading to the realization of your hopes. It's important to grasp the idea that our thoughts and actions emit a specific energy or vibration. People who are in sync with this energy will naturally resonate with us. When you consistently emit this energy, they will respond in kind. Life is a continuous exchange of energy among individuals, and your daily efforts contribute to building connections with different aspects of creation.

Your inner purpose comes from a part of our existence. It rewards you for all the good things you do. Something loved you even before you were born and brought you into this world. It has been with you since your birth. Even when you couldn't take care of yourself, it was there to give you all the love you needed. It continued to look after you every day until you became who you are today. So, how can you fail when you've done your part correctly?

There's a whole wide world out there, like a powerful magnet, always ready to bring your thoughts and cherished dreams closer to your heart, making them come true. It constantly tugs at you, urging you to create and turn your deepest desires into reality. Our ideas are akin to babies, conceived in a particular moment and destined to be born at a specific time. So, whatever you've been thinking till now doesn't matter as much as what's destined to become a reality.

If you've been trying to fit into a regular situation, then as you continue to progress, that's what you can expect in the future. If you haven't clearly defined your role in that situation, you can still continue to become what you truly adore. The ultimate result of everything is determined by our most profound thoughts, our deepest desires, and what we genuinely seek in creation. So, when you make efforts, don't just dip your toes in what you truly want to see happen; instead, make sure that your deepest soul's desires are what you hold close to your heart.

The complexity of your goal determines how much dedication you must invest. If you had simply chosen to lead a typical life, perhaps everything would have been clear. However, you consistently reject the notion of being ordinary and strive for a place where you truly belong. Now, significant changes have occurred, unveiling a grander vision, and you must find your role within it.

It appears that you had the option to decline becoming an ordinary individual because the world is summoning you. If you aren't decisive, it might be uncertain where you truly belong. Are you a member of the everyday society, or has your heart discovered a dwelling place among the stars? Once you have accurately answered that question, you can find your rightful place.

If you're aiming to be a part of the regular world, everything that makes you who you are should find its place in your work life. Any ideas you have should be compatible with this space where you discover your true self. This is where our lives start to take shape and acquire a meaningful purpose that makes being a human worthwhile.

When we discover our rightful place in the world, we gain the opportunity to manifest our true inner selves, and our viewpoint becomes firmly rooted. Every aspect of your innate being remains relevant, no matter how extensive your wisdom may be. You've unearthed your sanctuary, establishing a foundational understanding that guides your responses to life's challenges. However, this truth may seem elusive at times, and you might have felt adrift. Nevertheless, you must harmonize your entire essence with a specific place, and comprehending this principle can be intricate, yet it represents a fundamental law of the universe.

There comes a moment in life when you should let go of many things in the world and become a part of something you genuinely comprehend. Everything truly comes to life when you perceive it through your personal experiences. You're either a genuine member of what you're presently involved in, or you find yourself without a place at all.

Understanding oneself is not always easy, but you shouldn't dismiss the idea. It won't lead to any growth. Ensure your personal development continues until you reach a transformative stage. Discover your true self and find contentment in all that you need to be. The world provides a solid foundation, and you might need a strong idea to navigate it. If you truly wish to see your deepest thoughts manifest, you might have to go beyond the ordinary where many others reside. While it may not always define your identity, it's how things will ultimately make sense in the end.

You don't just need to understand what you're doing, but you also need to believe in the idea that forms your perspective. Because until you reach your destination, a part of who we are is driven by our individual motivations. We can all follow the same path, but we might be aiming for different outcomes. So, what you do with your abilities defines how much you love that specific thing. The roles others play in your life will eventually end, leaving you with your true self. Therefore, for a dependable journey, you must recognize that you are primarily responsible for your actions.

There are many ways we can help each other, but there comes a point when you must journey alone. No one can live your life for you, no matter who you are. Being human means accepting our responsibilities as we move forward, as there is no one else who can do it for us.

At the core of our being, each of us is distinct as human beings. Everything we engage in should adhere to this fundamental truth. Embracing our differences holds great value, for life is a dynamic exchange of human energy. We possess unique qualities that we must share with one another, and it is imperative that we recognize these distinctions. This recognition is essential to the creative process; thus, it is incumbent upon us to contribute something novel to what is presently accessible.

If I know what you have, I might not be too excited to see it. It can be a pleasant surprise when you present something different from what everyone was anticipating, even if we're all in the same situation. Sometimes, we may not be exceptionally creative on our own, but when we collaborate, we can come up with meaningful ideas. However, it doesn't make much sense if everything we do is just like what others are doing. So, as we work together, we can break down the barriers of understanding and achieve something truly remarkable.

If you're not able to do a lot by yourself, it's a good idea to help each other achieve your dreams. When people work together as a team, they can build their dreams together. By staying in touch with others, you can satisfy your desire for success and help each other reach your goals. Sometimes, when a group of people with different ideas comes together, they can create something amazing. This is because each person in the group has their own unique thoughts and talents.

Perhaps you find yourself in a unique position, seeing the world through a different lens compared to many others. Your focus lies in pursuing your life's aspirations, and you've made the decision to shine brightly, becoming someone who engages with a broader realm of existence. Your desire to find a sense of home extends beyond the confines of traditional employment, as it doesn't fully fulfill your inner self. You yearn for more from life than just a workplace where your creative ideas are born; you long for a place where you truly belong.

You are like a brilliant star, shining so brightly that you cannot be contained within the boundaries of ordinary surroundings. You rise above all the stages and platforms of the world, yearning to radiate your unique light. You've discovered inspiration from the vastness of the world around you, and you've found harmony within yourself, embracing your true essence.

The moment has arrived for you to contribute your unique qualities. You shouldn't stay hidden; instead, become an active member of your community. Join the ranks of people who share the same existence as you. Think of yourself as a shining star, representing boundless potential. Your life is brimming with unexpected moments and hidden treasures. As an individual, you possess an abundance of untapped potential. All you need to do is discover it and share it with the world. Your particular talents and your connection to the broader universe are both valuable. You have the potential to make a meaningful impact on everything that exists.

No matter how much you may feel different from others, there's always a part of you that shares similarities with someone else. There's a common thread that runs through all of us, and it's important to acknowledge that no one has had a completely smooth journey in life. Understanding the reasons behind your past struggles can help you grasp why you haven't achieved your goals thus far. Recognizing these challenges is the first step toward realizing the importance of wholehearted commitment. It's crucial not to remain ensnared in darkness, as everyone has traveled a similar path on their way to success.

Nobody was born there, or just to naturally belong to the stage. This should be one of the reasons you must ensure that you always remember it's a world where a lot is shaped by your own hard work and desires. It's important that you comprehend precisely what's expected of you. Afterward, play your role, nurture your ideas until they're fully developed, and align yourself with a meaningful concept. Understand that you're embracing your newfound identity. Eventually, someone or something that resonates with the same idea will come along and embrace you for all the love you carry within you.

Now, as we find ourselves in this world with many things to experience as humans, and as you've explored the vastness of existence, you may have faced challenges in discovering your true self. However, if being a star resonates with you in a way that makes you feel it's your destiny, don't hesitate to embrace it. Even though we may be in competition with others, a part of your essence remains undisturbed, as if it naturally belongs right there.

You are present to find your place among others, and you won't be the pioneer in your category. Your purpose is to enhance a specific concept or an existing world that shares similar principles, aspirations, and a clear purpose with yours. Once you've fully formulated your ideas and completed all your preparations, this environment will acknowledge your contribution and offer the support you need.

You can go to many different places around the world, knocking on doors and seeking acceptance or trying to make others see things from your perspective. However, not everything you receive from the outside world will suffice. It's essential to start by cultivating these qualities within yourself. You'll realize when you've reached the point where you truly deserve to be. This is akin to standing on a robust platform that makes your aspirations attainable, regardless of the many questions that may arise along the way.

If you find that things are challenging, don't worry. Eventually, you can become the solution to your own wishes. Develop a strong trust in yourself as you work towards your most cherished goal. Don't come up with reasons for not reaching your goals. You must have put in a lot of effort by yourself, and be confident that you are built on an idea that won't fade even if others abandon it. Understand that you are the solid base of your own creation, firmly established and unbreakable. You may face setbacks at various levels, but always stand firm in your vision for yourself.

Chapter Fifteen

Power over Money

Once you reach the point of achieving success, you have the freedom to select what aligns best with your desires. This is because, without any pretense, you are engaging in all the possibilities that are accessible to us as human beings. It's impossible to ignore the reality that you, too, are one of those individuals whose decisions on this planet are shaped by all the things that motivate people in life.

Sometimes, you might feel the urge to trade your creation for cash, as this temptation affects everyone. It can lead you to seize any chance that comes your way. Nevertheless, if you originally aimed to reach a specific aspiration, you should allow that overarching purpose to shape your entire existence and guide your ultimate choices.

In the end, what will truly count is your ability to demonstrate patience while striving to attain your deepest desires, particularly when you possess a brilliant idea. Throughout your journey, you will encounter numerous alluring opportunities, but you will also face substantial obstacles that challenge your pursuit of your lifelong ambitions.

However, it's important to remember that you can't hold human beings responsible for obstructing your path when they're merely attempting to be a part of your vision, even if unintentionally. You are the visionary; you have the responsibility of carrying the goals and objectives of your desired achievement. Nobody else can live out your vision on your behalf. Sometimes, it might be necessary for you to assertively pursue your objectives, and you should have confidence in your understanding of what you're doing.

Being assertive means showing a strong desire to achieve your deepest goals. When you insist on demonstrating your understanding and intentions clearly, you can become a highly influential individual through your creative endeavors.

The path you choose to travel should provide all the things you need to keep you safe from everything around you. Even if the goal you want to achieve seems very complicated, if it helps human beings, then nothing can stop it from happening. Along the way, you'll encounter various situations, but some of them will clearly show whether what you're doing is harmful or helpful to the world. To succeed, ensure that your actions are not solely focused on yourself and your goals; instead, let people be a central part of what you aim to achieve.

In everything we do, there's a special point that you reach when you continue moving forward. This point exists in your life, and it's where your inventions or ideas start to guide themselves. When you reach this level, you've unlocked the path to success, and there's no turning back. Everything you are keeps advancing. While the challenges you face to reach this point can be tough, once you arrive, many things become easier.

Achieving complete understanding can be tough. Over time, you might face challenges that seem like setbacks. People around you might wonder why things aren't clear to them. Since these are the people you live with, they could be really worried about how you manage things or your actions. If you try to explain yourself, it might not make sense because we live in a world where you might be the only one who gets what you're doing. But that doesn't mean you should feel bad about yourself if not everyone understands you.

You have the ability to dwell within your thoughts without any restrictions, allowing yourself to truly believe in the reality you desire to witness unfolding before your eyes. This freedom empowers you, never holding you back. You persist, assured that you harbor no regrets about attempting to conform to conventional understanding. Instead, you revel in the immense satisfaction derived from residing in the world you've constructed through your own comprehension. The paramount achievement is to exist within your innermost self, where you possess unwavering conviction in all your endeavors, extending to the very core of your existence. Your contentment knows no bounds as you remain fully convinced that whatever it is you aspire to bring into existence will ultimately fulfill your ardent desire to become the embodiment of your true passions.

In the depths of your heart, you should feel complete and satisfied with whatever it is you live for. Your mind and soul should be calm and peaceful, within your grasp. When you achieve this inner serenity, external influences won't have the power to bewilder you. This is one of the wonderful aspects of being your authentic self and living your unique life. Once you've built a sanctuary within yourself where all that you hold dear coexists harmoniously, the world won't be able to divert your attention or persuade you otherwise. You'll have the ability to steer the course of your own destiny.

The truth that everyone accepts cannot impact who you are and how you make decisions. Therefore, you can keep developing your ideas until they achieve success. People are different from each other, and what matters to you might be everything. When you observe the world, others may see something else, but for you, it could be the meaningful life you seek. It's important to stay true to yourself and your values, even when others try to persuade you otherwise, while you strive to fulfill your unique purpose.

Since we have the opportunity to come into this world at various moments in history, our perspectives may differ. Therefore, if you successfully accomplish your goals, it can convey a great deal about your significance in the grand scheme of existence, particularly in this modern century where countless individuals are highly motivated to excel in their endeavors.

To succeed, it's crucial to fully grasp the importance of your actions and discover where your skills are in high demand. Recognize that even if someone tries to hinder your path to success, the world relies on what you provide. When a substitute for your contributions emerges, people will opt for it, potentially leaving you with an unsatisfactory life.

Sometimes, life can become challenging to handle. This difficulty might lead to unfavorable outcomes, especially if you're not excelling in what you're pursuing. You may attempt to rectify the situation, but your efforts might not yield any positive results. It could even feel like your efforts are slowly fading into obscurity.

However, if you focus on learning and improving your skills, you can avoid the negative consequences of incompetence in your creative endeavors. As you progress, you'll come to realize that successful ideas are the result of careful nurturing and dedicated effort.

Doing things correctly will bring you a sense of fulfillment because you'll be pleased with how things have turned out in your life, despite any confusion or setbacks. Therefore, when something new starts as part of the world's changing ways, don't deprive yourself of the victory. Keep in mind that being human means making a few mistakes, especially when you didn't realize that personal growth within the vast scope of creation often demands discipline.

Mistakes happen because people are not perfect. However, when you do things correctly, the outcomes can be long-lasting. Therefore, maintain a positive attitude and concentrate on moving forward with honesty. Much of what we do relies on common sense, and you can attain valuable success. It's important to recognize that having talent is just one part of the equation; applying your knowledge with discipline takes your understanding to the next level.

When you have completed tasks with great precision, there is no need to glance around, wondering whether you have executed everything exceptionally, or if there exists an entity responsible for the successful completion of your endeavors. The reward is undeniable, and you should patiently anticipate its arrival, for it will undoubtedly seek you out.

If you've completed your tasks as they should be done, then the question arises: upon whom do you place your trust? Who emerges as the dependable source from which you anticipate receiving something in return? Is it an entity capable of managing its own achievements, or is it necessary for your life to attain its utmost potential that you must depend on fellow human beings? Depending on your aspirations, this reliance can, in turn, significantly impact the final outcome of your desired objectives.

If your work hasn't been very productive, where do you find your purpose in life? When you complete a task, you give your all to make your dreams come true and see your understanding gain significance. So, who helps you emerge from that dark place?

You might have dedicated all your energy to a particular idea to make it happen. We must see our projects through to the end so that, when they succeed, they can remind us of our humanity. Now that you haven't achieved your dreams, it can be a chance to rediscover who you used to be before starting this journey. Who can guide you back to your former self?

Creativity is the process of working on something until it starts to make sense in your life and the world around you. When you keep trying and pushing yourself, you can create something new and valuable. It's about making your ideas a reality, even if they seem impossible at first. It's like building a bridge between the past and the future, and it's worth your time and effort. Even when things get tough, finding satisfaction in being creative is a special gift.

The real exchange is forever between the inventor and what they invent. They both have value, and the creator brings their invention to life by showing it to the world. In return, it unlocks new opportunities for humanity. It's not just important once, but it has always been the most important thing to remember that you should work hard to shine a light on everything you do or hope to see. This way, you can truly experience what it means to be human.

If you always hold back and don't fully invest yourself, all your hard work may end up going to waste. You don't have to dwell on the past; just remember that when you wholeheartedly contribute to a specific idea, you're likely to receive something valuable in return. By sharing your thoughts and making your voice heard, you enable your ideas to take shape and reach places you might not have imagined. It's challenging to advocate for something that can't speak for itself. Without your efforts, you might not have accomplished anything, but you've dedicated your one and only life to realizing a particular vision in the way you believe it should be achieved.

Perhaps, you may not have fully grasped the importance of being meticulous right from the start. All you understand is that this is how an idea should be carefully cultivated. Thus, if something truly remarkable is destined to occur, it will gradually come to you as you continue progressing and advancing in your creative journey.

Not achieving success early on in your journey can lead you to become deeply immersed in various activities. You may find yourself growing frustrated with the tasks you're undertaking, all while being acutely aware that you've devoted a significant portion of your youth to pursuing a particular goal. As you progress along this path, you might ponder and daydream about the myriad possibilities that could have unfolded had you not committed yourself to this particular endeavor.

Sometimes, you may encounter moments when you grapple with comprehending why you embarked on endeavors like these. Yet, gradually, you come to recognize that many aspects of existence lacked significance until you embraced this lifestyle. Consequently, as you traverse the path of exploring the world, you undergo a profound transformation, evolving into an individual imbued with a genuine sense of purpose, one directed towards the act of creation.

The world you currently understand has merged with your consciousness, making you sense the universe within your entire existence. In the past, you had no knowledge of your true self until you embarked on this voyage. It was as if you were ineffectual in every circumstance you encountered. As you began to perceive your own worth, it was a result of your newfound dedication to excel in every challenge presented to you. It was through this sense of purpose that you found the strength to confront all the obstacles in your path.

For a man who might have wanted to travel with a special person, you might feel quite sad because, at this moment, you're only living to fulfill some of your needs. Without genuine love, you can't be entirely happy. When you reach this point in life, you become like an island, always alone with no one around to look after you. You sit there by yourself, and no one understands what you're doing, and there's nothing anyone can do to assist you.

Deep inside your heart and soul, there's a strong desire to find happiness. But you're unsure about how to let someone get closer to you because your work always takes precedence. Achieving contentment is crucial, and you believe that getting things right in your career is the key to obtaining all your desires. Perhaps this will also pave the way to meeting someone who holds true love in their heart. Unfortunately, the downside is that your sense of self-worth seems to hinge on your professional success. While you cherish the aspiration of becoming the greatest, you must be cautious not to let your ambitions turn you into a recluse, living in isolation indefinitely. Remember, this world is inhabited by both men and women, and nobody is granted the privilege of pushing themselves to the limit unless they are absolutely confident that they will return with success in all aspects of life.

When you've spent a long time working and waiting to display your talent, and now you're filled with eagerness to bring your work into the spotlight, it may be necessary to distance yourself from distractions and focus on perfecting your skills. Even though you can't showcase everything you've learned all at once, many things will take shape as you continue on your journey. Remember, this is the only life you have, no matter how overwhelming the need for precision and extra attention may feel. The person you become is your only path to being human and achieving success through your understanding. So, your preparations are meant to ensure you don't disappoint yourself.

You exist to embrace the opportunities that the world offers as you endeavor to grow, and you experience great satisfaction in understanding that when you actively pursue a goal, you're likely to discover the solution. Even when life gets tough, remember that on this planet, people are not meant to endure hardships while striving to embody their deepest passions.

Your patience, as you work hard to make others understand you, is an essential part of your daily existence. It serves as your refuge from the burdens that can weigh someone down while they continue to live on this Earth. To ensure you don't lose faith in yourself or in the tasks that are essential for your journey towards your goals, it's crucial not to allow your ambitions to slip away due to a lack of courage.

You have to realize that there will be things that you may not succeed at because they are not meant for you. This should inspire you to be brave as you follow the path where you discover your true self. On the flip side, it's important to understand that you can't afford to fail at everything. When you have a clear goal, you must do everything necessary to achieve it. As human beings, we sometimes find it hard to let go of our past selves, so you need to let go of the old and embrace your new life. The sacrifices you make to reach your goals will eventually pay off when you reach the finish line.

To succeed and rise above those who simply seek knowledge and self-awareness, it's important to strive for excellence. Instead of just entertaining fleeting thoughts, concentrate on achieving your goals, as your future depends on it. If you don't succeed after investing significant time, it could harm your identity. Show unwavering determination and embrace your desired path, as people prefer honesty and don't want to be deceived or exploited. So, if you possess ample knowledge, you hold the key to surpass those who only aim for awareness of the world's happenings and its future direction.

As you strive with true comprehension and heightened concentration towards your objectives, you can attain what may appear to be the most challenging to attain. Desiring something and achieving it, then sustaining a respectable livelihood from it, can seem effortless, yet it is not. It demands your complete essence to ascend to a particular point where your entire existence finds purpose in being labeled as a life. You might have embarked on this journey believing success would be straightforward; however, it is far from simple.

It becomes easier when you've faced and overcome life's challenges. Sometimes, the simplest ideas can be grasped swiftly after thorough learning, requiring considerable effort before they become effortless.

When you reach the end of your journey in pursuing your goals, you can start living a simpler life because you've created a path you can follow. Working hard and staying committed will help you avoid unnecessary tasks and focus on what truly matters. Why engage in things that don't align with your goals when you aim for success in a straightforward way?

You had love and responsibilities that you should have taken care of when you were younger, but you didn't give them enough attention. Now that you're older, you're facing the consequences of your actions, and there's no one left to support you. So, as you move forward, you should ask yourself where you can find a meaningful relationship in this difficult situation. Perhaps there's still something wonderful waiting for you in life if you're determined to achieve the goal that resides deep within your soul. If you embrace the challenge and succeed, things can improve in every aspect of your life.

Life might have been simpler, but now that you've committed yourself to so many tasks and responsibilities, everything has taken an unexpected twist. It's challenging to find a clear path where opportunities can come your way. However, if you manage to conquer the challenges that confront you, things may start to fall into place and make sense.

You could have obtained anything you desired under regular circumstances. But what if you didn't grasp how to perform tasks promptly? There was room for someone to join your life, so you could learn and grow together. However, you chose not to follow that path and be different from others. The unfortunate aspect is that you can't return to your previous self. Now, you're all by yourself, and you're aware that it takes a considerable amount of time for things to transform and adapt to their ideal state.

The delay can make you feel like things aren't going as planned, or perhaps they are, but we struggle to hold onto our beliefs. You desire for everything to occur naturally, without the need for coercion, yet now you've shifted away from your core essence, undergoing significant changes in your being. Therefore, when you ponder whether it's necessary to exert extra effort to bring your desires to fruition, the response is affirmative; you may indeed need to exert considerable effort to transform your aspirations into reality.

You shouldn't always wait indefinitely for things to become clear. Instead, you must take hold of opportunities and be true to yourself. Don't allow your desires to stop you forever. Even when you face unfamiliar situations and encounters, don't let your own ambitions imprison you. As you move forward, concentrate on understanding that even though you haven't faced these challenges before, now that your entire being relies on them, you will strive your hardest to overcome them.

Even when the result transforms you into someone entirely new, considering that it will require your full essence to navigate to the opposite shore, it seems as though these are scenarios devised by people solely to hinder your progress. At a certain juncture, you pledge that circumstances were never intended to unfold in this manner, as they do not appear to be heading in the direction of comprehension and achievement that you aspired to join.

In many aspects of your life, you display change in how you approach things. However, amidst these transformations, there remains a core similarity, a connection to others. As you progress toward your goals, you may find your world becoming more solitary, as few can truly comprehend or connect with the person you are becoming. It's undeniable that you feel the weight of living without the love and understanding of those in your immediate circle.

If you continue living the way you currently understand, you may eventually realize that you can achieve something meaningful in the end. The key is to keep strengthening your belief in the path you're following, no matter what challenges you face along the way. The more you persist and wholeheartedly commit yourself, the closer you'll come to a moment of self-discovery, where you recognize your significance in the larger scheme of things.

This is when the beauty of your thoughts will truly blossom and shine.

As time passes, it gradually brings forth the things you desire. The more time you spend doing a particular activity, the more expertise you gain in it. As a result, many aspects of the task start to unveil themselves, providing you with the ability to bring your actions into reality.

To stay focused and succeed as a human being, you need to develop a strong belief in yourself. This belief should empower you to approach challenging situations with a fresh perspective, even if you've faced failures before. With this self-assured belief, aim to become an expert in your chosen field. When you're confident in your abilities, you won't need to worry or panic. You won't have to rely on others to make things happen for you. Instead, you'll understand that your journey has equipped you with ample knowledge to shape your mindset and illuminate your future. This newfound confidence will enable you to thrive in any circumstance, no matter what challenges you may encounter.

No matter how much people say they know, sometimes they might not really grasp what you're doing. That's because they don't share your goals or have your vision. We all have our own dreams and plans for life and love hidden within us. You are the only one who truly understands your world; others can't see it the way you do. Trying to see things from someone else's point of view can be tough, and for some, it's almost impossible to see things the same way you do.

You have your unique vision, which is what you see in your mind. When you want to make something that many people can grasp easily, it means you need to look at things from a wider viewpoint. It can be challenging to comprehend what someone else is saying when they express their thoughts. The true meaning often becomes clear when everyone is working towards a common goal. Therefore, don't postpone the beauty of your creation. As you worry about reaching the end of your project, which you are actively involved in, you might overlook the crucial steps required to turn your goals into reality.

Don't ignore people or ensnare anyone with your thoughts. Strive to form a clear vision that everyone can grasp and find satisfaction in your creation. This can aid in shaping your aspirations and determining the extent of your impact on others' lives. Recognizing your intention to positively influence their welfare, remarkable outcomes may emerge from your efforts.

In the end, no matter what path we choose in life, we remain human beings. We must consistently strive to do our best in every situation, ensuring that we align with our chosen commitments and fulfill our purpose. If at any point you wish to revert to a previous path, you can do so. If the creative life feels unsuitable or too demanding, you have the option to step back. Life in the realm of creativity presents numerous challenges that may impact your endeavors. Nevertheless, if dedicating yourself to the process of bringing ideas to fruition is your true calling, then life will begin to take shape accordingly.

In everything we do, there's a particular commitment we should strive for.

This commitment helps us understand what we're doing. Having faith in this commitment allows good things to come into your life. This is especially true when you deeply care about your goals. When we start our journeys, we don't have all the knowledge we need. But as you move forward, you'll gain the knowledge necessary for future success.

As you progress in your pursuit of personal growth, you'll discover a crucial truth: knowledge is the key. If you have confidence in your actions and don't doubt yourself, that's all you require to ascend to a level where you can truly grasp the art of becoming a successful innovator. Along your journey, you may encounter individuals and situations resistant to change, but if you maintain unwavering belief, you can pave a path even in the darkest of times.

In life, perfection is not a necessity. Many people might not comprehend you as they ought to. However, if you find complete contentment within yourself, you become self-sufficient, not reliant on anyone's endorsement. When you are alone, you possess the ability to transform everything into something truly remarkable that no one can ever deny or obstruct in the way you envision.

We've reached a place in the world where folks have placed their faith in incorrect notions. Consequently, they've started assuming they possess complete knowledge about everything, resulting in significant failures. The truth is, when you sense something isn't correct, you don't necessarily need to persuade others. Even if you put in a lot of effort to correct it later, some things remain unchangeable. It becomes clear that you should have given more attention to the basics, as there are aspects we can adjust, while some endure indefinitely.

However, if you engage in an argument because you believe that you cannot alter the current state of affairs, it is akin to asserting that your past actions were justified. You may encounter individuals of this sort, who may attempt to influence your perspective with their opinions until you are compelled to adopt faith in your own knowledge. This is when you come to realize the significance of consistently pursuing the very vision you wish to endure, as opposed to entertaining thoughts and actions that diverge. What truly makes a positive impact is taking the correct course of action, rather than merely discussing or contemplating it, and anticipating others to conform or modify their viewpoints to align with yours.

Most of the time, you might find yourself wanting others to comprehend and embrace your actions and beliefs. However, they often prefer to maintain their own paths, even if those paths conflict with yours. You feel a deep conviction in persuading them to adopt your perspective because you firmly believe their beliefs are incorrect. Yet, they remain steadfast, unwavering in their ways. They choose to rely on what they have to handle the challenges they face, while within you, a strong conviction persists that your path is correct, and you wish for others to follow your lead, as you have faith in your own creations.

They are living their lives as usual, following the paths they've become accustomed to because that's where they've found meaning in their current existence. What they demonstrate is that it can be a lengthy process to adapt to a new way of life, particularly when you're unsure of where it's leading.

If you have a vision, you must be willing to take risks, even if you're not entirely sure of your destination. However, you should reassure yourself that you will discover who you can become on this journey, as long as you stay true to an honest and meaningful path that leads you toward personal growth. You may have realized that you haven't achieved your desired goals as quickly as you hoped, but this is the path you've chosen because it aligns with your beliefs. Regardless of the challenges that may appear daunting, you have faith that it will ultimately lead you to something truly wonderful.

You should always maintain a strong focus on doing what's right because sometimes people might present you with seemingly uncomplicated and less intricate options. However, deep down, you understand that these choices don't align with your true desires and the way things should ideally unfold, especially in terms of your personal aspirations. So, if you decline such offers, it doesn't mean you're insisting on your own path exclusively; it simply reflects your certainty that these alternatives do not reflect your true self or hold significance in relation to your ultimate goals.

Sometimes, we might choose something that seems good in the moment, but it can end up causing problems later on. The important thing is that our decisions should always protect what's best for us. We shouldn't be afraid of making mistakes or doing things that aren't exactly right; our fear comes from how it might affect the things we care about most. Our actions in relationships also play a role in protecting them. So, when you strive to do what's right, you'll attract someone who values honesty. True love is built on something genuine within us, and anyone who enters our life will follow that same path.

Perhaps, a lot of events and experiences have unfolded to lead to this current situation. It might have seemed like everything was against you in your pursuit of success as a wise individual with strong values. Nevertheless, you made a conscious decision to forge your unique path forward. This is the moment when it's crucial to hold onto your beliefs and maintain the integrity that resides within you. By doing so, you are actively shaping your own future. Therefore, when you find yourself lacking knowledge in a particular area, it begs the question: where do you place your trust, and what actions should you take in response to this?

You often find yourself caught up in life's challenges and circumstances. The key is to gain an understanding of the world around you and your actions. It's not enough to merely exist as a human being; you should strive to live in a way that reflects your vitality. This is a quality that defines you when you reach the end of your journey. When faced with difficult situations, you can rely on this guiding principle, whether it's a belief you've developed or something inspired by someone who created something remarkable. Embrace it and find contentment in it, as it shapes your identity. So, if you cling to your ideas in a world full of complexities, can you really blame yourself if you sometimes feel like you're lagging behind?

While you may firmly cling to your beliefs, there's no need to be afraid. Eventually, you'll find the ability to influence the course of events in your favor. This is especially true after dedicating a considerable amount of time and effort. So, even when time is passing, would you consider compromising your values for something you neither comprehend nor see the reason to surrender to?

Many times, you'll come to realize that despite your expectations, things may not turn out as you had hoped. You may reach a destination only to discover that your initial desires didn't materialize as you had envisioned. In such moments, you must continue forward as if you have no specific outcome in mind. However, in the end, you'll find that you've been pursuing your unique path, and the knowledge you've gained through experience will be crucial for ensuring accuracy and confidence in your endeavors. Therefore, endeavor to become an expert and excel in all that you undertake, recognizing that your life is a journey against the entire world. Ensuring your understanding aligns with reality is paramount.

Who ever said that you must receive formal instruction to reach a point where you excel in your passion for life? Perhaps you have the ability to shape your own vision into flawless fruition. After all, who could better understand the ultimate outcome than you? Moreover, who asserted that you must be guided step by step to achieve expertise in your creation? There exists a realm where your ideas can metamorphose into something utterly incomprehensible to others, and you possess the unique capability to bring it to life precisely as you envision.

Once you've completed all the necessary tasks, as long as you don't turn back, you will eventually achieve success. You might face confusion during your journey, but eventually, you will grasp the knowledge needed to reach your goals. Stick to your path for all your requirements because no one understands your vision better than you do. So, why would you work without a clear direction? The key is that you don't need to possess complete knowledge about the process of creation; what you require is faith. With faith, you can accomplish the seemingly impossible.

You exist within a vision crafted by your own imagination, and you are the ideal individual for whatever awaits you in the future. Every time you gaze beyond your surroundings, you possess a clear sense of your place in the world, even though you may not always fully take advantage of it. Nevertheless, it is crucial that you consistently pursue your endeavors with precision, for this is the essence of life in the grand scheme of things.

Chapter Sixteen

Enlarge Your Vision

When you observe the world, don't separate it into "them" and "you." Instead, view it as a vast platform where your desires can take shape. You also have an important role in bringing these desires to life. Never think that there are situations where your impact doesn't matter. In the grand tapestry of creation, there may come a moment where your contribution holds immense significance, even if it seems inconspicuous at first glance.

If you ever want to understand the price of becoming a part of everything in the world, then take your time. Dedicate yourself to something you truly want to achieve, like a goal or a specific objective. You'll be amazed because, without a doubt, you'll make progress towards it. Many people believe that a miracle will magically make their dreams come true, but that's not how it works. You must be fully aware of your actions and how you accomplish your goals.

You should let your strong determination guide you along the journey of creation because no extraordinary abilities or magic will simply fulfill your deepest desires without effort. It's essential to begin a project from its very beginning, care for it with unwavering dedication, be patient, and provide it with opportunities to flourish. Your persistent affection for it will eventually transform it into a work of art, and when the right moment comes, it will undoubtedly materialize.

Every single thing in this world has a start, a point when it begins its journey. Sometimes, it all kicks off from absolutely nothing at all. Yet, as the clock keeps ticking, you have the potential to evolve into something truly incredible, something that leaves people in awe. But here's the question: how much effort do we need to invest for our aspirations to transform into a magnificent reality? It's a puzzle without a clear answer because the right amount of dedication can be a moving target, and there's no way to predict when your dreams will transform into a work of art.

While striving for a meaningful life is your ultimate destination, it's possible to become disoriented during the journey due to the complexity of gaining precise understanding. From the moment we are born, we possess unique qualities, but now you have the opportunity to transform yourself into a new version, all in pursuit of realizing your ultimate aspiration. Shifting your attention away from external distractions can contribute significantly to excelling in your desired goal.

Perhaps you've often pondered, deep within your thoughts, about the unique talents and abilities you might possess. It can be frustrating when you feel like you're falling short of your potential. However, if you genuinely desire to uncover your inner magic, you need not search far and wide. The truth is, you already possess all you need, and it's your unwavering determination to excel in your pursuits that will unlock even greater opportunities. Remember, nothing will come your way unless it aligns with your desires. The key to this enchantment lies in embracing your inherent gifts. Within you lies a remarkable essence, a core identity that has been with you since birth, waiting to be fully acknowledged and celebrated.

Every individual possesses a unique quality that distinguishes them from others. Even when hidden within, if there were a contest, that particular aspect of your character would undoubtedly emerge as the ultimate victor. It serves as the reigning champion within our existence, functioning as the focal point of creativity and harboring boundless potential within ourselves.

It all starts as a tiny speck, like a single grain of sand, and it gradually expands as you care for it with unwavering dedication. If you truly wish to unearth your inner greatness, you may find it necessary to center your attention on the facet that corresponds to your deepest understanding of who you are. This can offer you valuable insights into the actions you should take, as it perpetually resides within you and forms the basis of your regular interactions. You persistently hone your skills to become the best version of yourself, for knowledge is your weapon to confidently confront the challenges of the world. As you venture into the realm of reality, you'll encounter formidable competition.

You can learn a lot, but sometimes it's hard to decide what to focus on. To do well, you should be the best at something you know. You must stand out and shine. Maybe you have knowledge that hasn't helped you yet, but if you broaden your view, you could make something incredible. Think about what you love most about yourself, and you might discover something magnificent. Imagine all the knowledge you have and how it relates to the universe and everything we know.

Each of us possesses a side that leans toward concentration and interpretation, reacting to everything we encounter to understand the world around us. This should be our primary focus when addressing various situations. Perhaps this perspective can provide you with a more insightful understanding of how things work. It not only aspires to lead but also embraces responsibility for achieving success. Therefore, maintaining concentration on this aspect is essential, regardless of the other priorities that may demand our attention.

There are many things that can help you learn more about our world as humans. If you choose one of these things and use it to look at the whole world, it can become very meaningful. Think of yourself as a compass with four directions, or maybe even more than that. Whatever direction you focus on will bring out the best in you as a person. So, when you decide which way to go, make sure it leads to something you really love about yourself, as there might not be a chance to change course later on.

At times, it's important to concentrate on various matters, including matters of the heart, and this can become quite meaningful at specific moments. When you're seeking something, it's vital to be deeply immersed in your pursuit, particularly when it pertains to aspects that unite us as humans. This is because without focused effort, you might not make any headway, and being immersed in your goals is essential.

It really depends on how your life has been treating you up until now. If things have been going smoothly, you might want to consider continuing down that path. Making a commitment to someone may have already proven beneficial for you, so it's worth sticking with it. You shouldn't easily give up on such a valuable connection. It's not common for a person to fully dedicate themselves to another, and you might find it necessary to continue in that direction. Who knows, something truly wonderful could unfold as you journey along this path.

You can start from scratch or with just about anything. By broadening your view and concentrating on your goals, you can draw towards yourself all that you want. Remember that, no matter how we feel, everything we encounter plays a crucial role in the world around us. These things can be ideas created by anyone's mind, originating from the simplicity of thoughts. You too can embark on this journey for yourself, initiating your own endeavor and pursuing it towards the pathway to success.

You have the ability to view the world from various angles, each of which holds significance in the realm of human experience. Whether you contemplate aspects like love, life, money, or family, there is inherent value in all these facets of our existence, along with any other positive elements you might seek. So, regardless of the path you choose to focus on, you are bound to discover something worthwhile. However, it can be challenging to maintain concentration when numerous distractions vie for your attention. Why is it necessary to keep your mind fixed on a specific direction? Perhaps it's because until you become proficient in a particular sphere of existence, you may not fully reap the benefits of this world and what it offers you.

You can attempt it, but the world will constantly tug you in various directions until you master the art of deep focus on your true desires. Once you've decided how you want to face reality, it might prove challenging to uncover your talents or identify the passion that brings out your best self. Achieving early certainty about your chosen path is a valuable gift, requiring discipline and a deep understanding of yourself. With such clarity, navigating the complexities of creation becomes simpler, enabling you to expand your influence on a global scale.

You have the power to shape yourself based on what captures your attention. Your origins may lie within your family, and you have the potential to inherit a business and transform it into a lasting legacy. By integrating it into your creative endeavors, you can share its brilliance with the world, providing opportunities for others to benefit. It is often said that if you invest your time and deep focus, you can create something truly extraordinary as a human being. Your productivity hinges on which aspect of yourself you feel most inspired by. If you draw strength from managing household matters, use that as a foundation to nurture your ambitions. Anything that fuels your passion has the potential to evolve into a remarkable masterpiece.

The key thing to consider is that you've taken a thorough look in every direction, examining where you might fit in and become a valuable individual. Within you, there must exist a facet that is characterized by strength, concentration, and productivity. This facet is what enables you to thrive in this world. Even if you've been leading a relatively comfortable life, you may still lack the vital essence of existence because you haven't made clear decisions about your preferred way of doing things. It's possible that no aspect of your being has solidified, leaving you feeling trapped regardless of the path you choose to follow.

It seems like you've been facing a lot of stress lately, and it's been quite a while. You can't keep going in circles; you need to find stability. You must grasp something meaningful in the various aspects of our lives. To truly become a human being, you must strive to understand things.

Love can be a significant force in your life when you genuinely embrace it. Breaking through obstacles doesn't always revolve around the hardships you faced in grasping a particular aspect of existence. You need not make sacrifices in pursuit of extraordinary desires; instead, you can wholeheartedly devote yourself to cherishing that unique individual until the cosmos unveils a plethora of boundless opportunities.

Engaging in such actions can unlock a unique trait within a person. If you dedicate yourself to broadening this concept, many individuals may grasp it and discover aspects of themselves through it. While it's often said that love is like an invisible force guiding us, it's essential to remember that we cannot remain oblivious indefinitely. If you've been fixated on this particular aspect, the world cannot disregard its significance. Eventually, we must prioritize our survival; we cannot constantly center our lives around one another. We must also savor life's moments.

You should allow things to come to you because the world needs love every day. We could use some assistance from people with different viewpoints. Think about how it would impact our world if love spread globally through you. It's a rare quality in this modern age. Often, we neglect self-care and suffer as a result of not sharing our true selves. We never knew that such dedication could be a key ingredient for achieving remarkable feats or improving people's lives.

We often don't think of our relationships as something that might lead to more. We find it difficult to understand the world beyond our immediate surroundings. We don't take the time to expand our point of view, even though it could be crucial. It might even be your safe haven, where you reside in your familiar world. So, don't simply harbor love in your heart indefinitely without realizing that it could be a gateway to greater things. If you truly wish to experience greatness, take steps to prepare yourself. No matter how you perceive things, if you can concentrate deeply, you can observe many positive outcomes returning to you.

The idea here is that when we concentrate on specific aspects of reality, it helps us bring out our finest qualities. By consistently dedicating our attention to a single subject until we attain mastery, we can achieve excellence in our comprehension of that area. We can then further develop and broaden our expertise, sharing our vision with the global community and earning recognition for our accomplishments.

Nobody can discriminate against you when you do something essential using your unique skills and knowledge. Some people may argue that our motivation is driven by the rewards we receive, but we've put in the effort to become experts. You shouldn't be judged for your perspective; that's a fundamental aspect of being human. Imagine having money, which isn't typically associated with innovation, and having a vision to achieve greatness with it. This idea also holds a lot of merit, as it's a crucial element in pursuing any endeavor.

With such a substantial amount of money, you have the opportunity to kickstart your business and bring your dreams to life. However, it's important to understand that handling a large sum of money can be quite challenging. You might obtain it, attempt to put it to good use, face difficulties in managing it effectively, and eventually lose it all. What you initially had could vanish, but this experience can be a valuable lesson in responsible money management. Ultimately, the quantity of money you possess may not be the most critical factor; rather, it's how you leverage it to enhance your knowledge and achieve greater things.

We possess various resources to face the world, and when it comes to business, money plays a pivotal role. It's indispensable for driving progress and achieving our goals. Business endeavors offer opportunities to shine, and even with a modest initial investment, one can amass substantial wealth. No one can fault you for your success; it simply reflects your adeptness in leveraging your assets.

You've put in a lot of effort to effectively run your business, and through your dedication, it has become quite successful. You've utilized your available resources to achieve your desired goals. Is that particular thing you're constantly fixated on truly so negative that you find it impossible to divert your gaze? It seems to be a permanent presence, so why not take control of it and transform yourself into whatever you aspire to become.

On the opposite side, we find life, and it presents a distinct perspective compared to all aspects of reality we encounter. It has perpetually posed the greatest challenge for humans to comprehend. This occurs when you observe things in existence externally and are capable of deciphering them independently, without the necessity of involving others or relying on the foundations of creation.

Understanding the true worth of life is not an easy task, and it requires a double dose of commitment to shield you from any challenges that may cross your path. In addition to all the tools you possess to face the world, this aspect holds greater significance than many other things in existence. There's something exceptional about employing our thoughts as a strategy that truly distinguishes it.

It provides you with inner protection, enabling you to perceive and comprehend potential issues. This is a fundamental rule that you should honor when attempting to grasp the intricacies of navigating the world. When everything you attempt appears to be going awry, there's no need to search elsewhere, as the solution lies within your grasp.

If you haven't completely learned about yourself in life, there might be times when you can't find the right path. Life safeguards us from potential problems, so it's crucial to learn the first rule of survival. Before you can benefit from your knowledge of the world, you should know how to protect yourself from potential dangers. What's even more challenging is that you're the one responsible for your creativity. Having a better understanding of ourselves and the world allows us to be the main creators of our ideas, enabling us to take the lead.

You are the creator of everything that grants you the essence of life. Anything can have a counterpart, like wealth, affection, and family. You have the potential to receive an inheritance of riches, require a companion in a romantic partnership, and possess the ability to perceive the world from your unique domestic vantage point, which can guide you towards the goals you aspire to manifest. Nevertheless, in our life journeys, we stand as individuals, and it is incumbent upon us to exert diligent effort to attain comprehensive comprehension of all that contributes to our overall welfare.

Initially, we often find ourselves in a state of being that serves as the fundamental building block for our understanding of the world. This foundational phase is crucial when pursuing a distinct goal independently. As you accumulate knowledge and expertise, you gain the capacity to ascend to higher levels of mastery in your pursuits, ultimately returning as a valuable and proficient individual.

You gain a profound understanding of a wealth of hidden knowledge, enabling you to overcome the multitude of negative thoughts within your mind and take control of your destiny. As a result, others can look to you as a timeless source of wisdom, a steadfast cornerstone upon which all your needs can be met. This enduring legacy endures through the ages, remaining unchanged and eternally relevant, serving as the fundamental bedrock for all your requirements.

You can improve your knowledge and skills to face the world confidently. By doing so, you can become successful and gain recognition on a global scale. Your expertise can lead to groundbreaking innovations as you learn everything required to excel. Ultimately, your journey will transform you into a symbol of beauty and excellence for everyone to admire.

Looking at life from this perspective, it becomes apparent that things often unfold in unique and unexpected ways. It appears that achieving success requires more than just a narrow focus solely on the end result, as it's not something handed to you; you must actively pursue it. To excel in your chosen path, you must seek to gain a deep understanding from various sources across the world and within diverse realms of knowledge. Our lives encompass a wide range of experiences and encompass everything. When you view the world as your stage and your goal is to gain acceptance from all that exists, there is no need to cultivate enmity; this approach serves as the doorway to fulfillment.

Life is more than just living normally. You start to grasp what truly connects all things, and becoming skilled in this is the foundation of creativity. This is how we become experts and expand our possibilities. At times, you may want to surpass the usual and become extraordinary. To do this, you must possess belief, and through it, you will emerge triumphant, even discovering your true place in the world.

While everything we experience becomes a familiar part of our lives, it's crucial to recognize the far-reaching consequences it may have. Some actions possess the potential to create significant global ripples while also posing potential pitfalls. The outcomes of our life experiences serve as valuable lessons, reminding us of our responsibility for our actions. We can't merely act without acknowledging the ripple effects, as every action resonates in some way with the fabric of reality. Therefore, it's essential to strive for excellence and aim to leave a positive mark on the world.

Feel thankful for everything that exists in the world. Remember, you're not the first person to be fascinated by the wonders of creation on this planet. Many individuals came before you, and they contributed to a vast reservoir of knowledge and experiences. You didn't just learn solely from your own abilities and insights; there was a rich tapestry of wisdom that had already paved the way for you to gain knowledge from.

What enables the possibility of all things? It is the creator and their boundless creativity, generously offering something fundamental to our very existence. It was the sole missing element. Once you've journeyed around the world, gaining profound insights through repeated exploration, it starts to converse with you. It becomes evident that everything is poised to transform you and establish a profound dwelling within the depths of your soul.

You are the endpoint, as you transform into the one who understands all that you have witnessed and endured throughout your life journey. When you thoroughly reflect on your experiences and derive positivity from them, you cease to be the same individual you once were; you are reborn as a fresh creation, and you embody knowledge in its purest form.

The second circle isn't exactly like the one you've already gone through. The first circle is all about understanding things in a physical way. However, it all depends on how deep the wounds in your soul are. You might need to broaden your view of life in a spiritual sense. This will help you pay attention to different aspects of yourself that might have been neglected for a long time. In the end, it becomes the everyday knowledge we all need to be truly human.

A person shaped by belief, leading a life that stands apart from the experiences of many. To those who've chosen to withhold the treasure of knowledge from themselves, what might the outcome be? Perhaps they haven't become shining stars, for a star symbolizes mastering the art of comprehending everything independently. This speaks volumes about our existence, both in our physical bodies and in the realm of the spirit. Physically, our journey entails grasping how to coexist harmoniously with fellow humans. On the spiritual plane, it's about discovering love in every entity that exists.

You gather the basic knowledge provided to you and expand upon it, making it much clearer for everyone to understand. Before everything becomes solidified, engage with various areas of knowledge and become proficient in everything that lies ahead of you. Pursue this for your own benefit so that anything trying to divert you from your path to success won't be able to do so easily. This will always be a challenge to your freedom, and it can have a significant impact on your well-being.

Sometimes, situations can become quite distressing, particularly when you've fully committed yourself to a particular idea and are determined to witness its fruition. You might find yourself in a state of great urgency, struggling persistently to grasp the intricacies of your pursuit, all in the relentless pursuit of achieving your desired objective. Nonetheless, when you possess unwavering confidence in your endeavors, you can find solace in the person you've evolved into, even in the face of inevitable setbacks and obstacles that may cause delays.

When things don't happen as you wish, and you can't ignore the reality that there are other individuals progressing in their life journeys, it can profoundly affect your sense of vulnerability. When people hold divergent viewpoints on matters that they are not well-informed about or that don't pertain to them, especially when you aspire to shine as a significant figure, someone who leaves a mark and derives fulfillment from it, it can be disheartening. When you devote yourself to everything around you, with the expectation of ultimately attaining happiness as the ultimate outcome, you come to realize that this pursuit is anything but straightforward.

When you take all your knowledge and transform it into something magnificent, you make even the simplest ideas bigger, so the whole world can appreciate them. People searching for guidance will discover it through you, while those seeking understanding will grasp it. Don't underestimate yourself; share your ideas with everyone. The universe yearns for your wisdom, and how will you convey everything you've witnessed? How will you contemplate the emotions you've experienced? Or perhaps, how will you vividly illustrate to the world how certain moments made you feel so vulnerable that tears welled up deep within you?

From across the globe, as I extend my reach, I wonder how you can connect

196

with what I'm attempting to convey – all the things I've witnessed. It might seem unrelated to what I initially wanted to share, but it's now become quite simple to explain, thanks to my current emotions. In this whole situation, my feelings have become deeply intertwined, and omitting them would be akin to committing a serious offense, something I'd struggle to make right.

While it might seem unnecessary to incorporate it into my job responsibilities, you definitely wouldn't want to jeopardize something as remarkable as this. The world is incredibly beautiful, and your desire is to inhabit it fully, ensure your contributions are acknowledged, but then, another obstacle unexpectedly disrupts this flow.

When you witness your dreams turning into reality, it can ignite a profound sense of excitement within you. As you pause to contemplate the sacrifices you've willingly undertaken, it becomes evident that these sacrifices were essential in your pursuit of a contented and fulfilling life. Consider the challenges you've boldly confronted, fully aware that they were necessary for your personal growth. Reflect on how you bravely shed your old self to make way for the emergence of a new, improved version of yourself. Remarkably, you've managed to withstand the pressures without succumbing to becoming someone you're not. This resilience safeguards you from making detrimental choices that could have adversely affected your well-being.

In certain circumstances, you may feel that you deserve something because you recognize when you've completed your responsibilities, and you're patiently waiting for the ideal moment to arrive and rescue you from any obstacles that may hinder your progress.

When you find yourself facing unexpected delays that you can't reverse, and you feel embarrassed in front of many people, even though you make efforts to catch up, circumstances won't make it easy for you. This situation eventually affects every aspect of your life. You can achieve your goals, but not on that particular platform anymore. You'll need to reach them on a different level, one that has always been your passion.

It's quite amusing how you've progressed through all the different phases of growth and comprehension in your unique manner. It's as if you've embarked on a journey to transform yourself into a shining star, someone who truly stands out amongst others and earns recognition for their exceptional talents. I wonder, how far do you think you can go in achieving this aspiration?

Have you ever considered the possibility of flipping your perspective completely and embracing the authentic and distinctive person that you are? It's about finding genuine happiness within yourself, a sense of joy that you truly desire. It's important to recognize that this joy is not some unattainable dream; it's very much within your reach. You simply aspire to let your inner light shine brightly and attain contentment with the knowledge you possess.

Have you ever thought about your role in the world? Can a single achievement unlock numerous possibilities? Does reaching one goal often pave the way for exciting new opportunities, guiding you along a distinctive journey that allows your potential to soar? Keep in mind that it's essential to feel content with the outcomes that unfold, having thoroughly considered all possible scenarios, and finding happiness in the results that emerge. When you embarked on your journey towards your destination, your primary goal was to find happiness within yourself at the journey's conclusion. Now that you have discovered this opportunity, embrace it with unbridled joy. Along the way, you encountered challenging situations that might have tempted you to take shortcuts, believing you had effortlessly sailed through them, but that wasn't the case. You navigated your journey admirably and courageously confronted every obstacle that arose. Sometimes, you even patiently awaited the fulfillment of your aspirations, and indeed, they eventually materialized.

Why aren't you feeling joyful about this? You possess remarkable qualities that have enabled you to turn your special talent into a reality. Additionally, you persevered through challenges and emerged victorious. You had this ability within you all along, and now you've demonstrated it to the world with exceptional success.

Don't just grapple with a small idea; put in effort to expand your knowledge and pursue the full scope of independence in human existence. Aim for that larger aspiration, rather than focusing on a small, insignificant goal that consumes your time. Seek something that genuinely fulfills your heart's desires instead of settling for mere contentment. A grand ambition is what you should dedicate your life to, one that liberates you eternally.

The End!!!

About the Author

Sibusiso Malvin Tshabangu Born 7 October 1986, South Africa. Studied at the Tshwane University Of Technology with a B Tech: Degree In Marketing. My books are solely based on my research which I have conducted for over twelve years, after completing my studies, which I later had a breakthrough in Pharmaceutical studies, which became my area of practice, however choose to focus mainly on life and relationships as a reflection of my understanding, which emphasizes on the fact that to avoid a lot of what we can define as diseases and medical disorders, man and woman should learn to focus on love, even if you can be a Master in life, on its own knowledge cannot do that much, love completes everything that we are.

Other Books by the Author

Inspiration About Life or Love

The Series Stars Do Fall in Love

1. Individualism

2. Fame

3. The Lady at the Center of my Heart